THE 2650 MILE AISLE

CAMERON JAMES WILLIAMS

CAMERON JAMES WILLIAMS

THE 2650 MILE AISLE

CAMERON JAMES WILLIAMS

Copyright © 2020 Cameron James Williams
All rights reserved. No part of this book may be reproduced, scanned, or distributed in any printed or electronic form without permission. Please do not participate in or encourage piracy of copyrighted materials in violation of the author's rights. Please purchase only authorized editions.

Print ISBN: 978-1-7353559-0-0
eBook ISBN: 978-1-7353550-1-7
Cover Design: Bilal Haider

THANK YOU!

Your purchase of this book matters. 25% of all the author's proceeds from *The 2650 Mile Aisle* are contributed to the American Diabetes Association (ADA). On behalf of anyone with friends, family members, neighbors—and certainly individuals—personally affected by diabetes: We say thank you!

CAMERON JAMES WILLIAMS

"Every hour of every day is an unspeakably perfect miracle." -Walt Whitman

TABLE OF CONTENTS

THE 2650 MILE AISLE iii

    THANK YOU! v

    PREFACE xi

    CHAPTER 1: INTRODUCTION 1

        Justin and Miranda at the Bridge 1

        The Announcement 11

        The Pacific Crest Trail 22

PART 1: PRE-MIRANDA 33

    Where It All Started 35

    CHAPTER 2: RESPECT IS EARNED; NOT GIVEN 39

        Meaning of an Older Brother 39

        Golden Ticket to the Backseat 50

        The Williams Name 54

    CHAPTER 3: A MAN AS A BOY 61

        Camping: A Call to the Wild 65

        Pushing the Limits of Intellect 76

        Pushing the Limits of Body 85

        Pushing the Limits of Willpower 88

    CHAPTER 4: THE ONLY WAY IS THROUGH 93

        Justin's Surprising News 101

        His Body is a Temple 109

- The Blemish Never Seen 113
- The Unsung Hero 117

CHAPTER 5: NEW BEGINNINGS 125

- Halloweekend 130
- Oh Captain, My Captain 138
- Fall Seven Times, Stand Up Eight 142
- Something Old and Something New 146
- Just Another Trophy on the Shelf 152
- Conclusion to Part 1: Pre-Miranda 156

PART 2: POST-MIRANDA 161

- Introduction 163

CHAPTER 6: A MATCH MADE IN (WHATEVER YOUR BELIEF SYSTEM) 171

- Welcome to the Party, Miranda 172
- Miranda, Meet Justin; Justin, Meet Miranda 178
- Winter Break: Plus One Edition   184
- No Rocky Meeting 193
- Acquired Taste 198

CHAPTER 7: ADVENTURERS AT HEART ... 209

- Broadening Their Horizon 214
- "Run, Justin (Forrest), Run" 219
- The Grand Proposal 223
- Welcome to Pure Michigan 229
- No Plan B 236

The Announcement (Again) 247
The Bracelet 252
Planning for the PCT 257
The Final Chat 263

CHAPTER 8: CONCLUSION 271

The Uncontrollable Virus 271
But They Can't Be Taken Away from Adventure
.... 277
The Best Man 279
You May Now Kiss the Bride 282

REFERENCES 287
ACKNOWLEDGEMENTS 297

CAMERON JAMES WILLIAMS

PREFACE

Traditionally, in formal weddings, the best man speech is a brief verbal address, presented by either a brother or close friend of the bridegroom (groom for short). Usually, the speech is to remain under five minutes—with the best man sharing an interesting or funny story about the groom and/or both newlyweds—ending with a toast as an expression of gratitude. But the soon-to-be marriage between my older brother, Justin, and his lovely fiancée, Miranda, is by no means usual. Normally, a large banquet center is rented out for the evening, a DJ is hired to play the *Cha-Cha Slide* and the other same ten songs you heard at the last wedding, and the choice of chicken or fish is offered as the entree for the attendees. Justin and Miranda's unique relationship lends itself to steer away from such a traditional wedding. Instead, in classic Justin and Miranda fashion, things will be done unconventionally; their way. Yes, they will be declaring their vows to each other. And yes, there will be a celebration of two separate individuals, families, and cultures uniting together as one. But not by any stretch of the imagination will either the marriage or wedding be viewed as 'normal' according to today's common culture, or perhaps any era for that matter. Partly, this 'going out on the limb' that I will describe in-depth shortly and throughout this entire book, is what makes their relationship—and Justin and Miranda as individuals—so noble and admirable.

Consequently, since the wedding will not be a 'copy and paste' of other weddings, I quickly realized a traditional best man speech would not be very fitting for the occasion. With an immense number of topics, ideas, and stories to discuss at the wedding party, it became evident to me that a five-minute timeframe would not suffice. And surely, I do not want to be considered 'that guy' who delivered a thirty-minute speech, as stomachs growl in expectation of a delicious meal; and as alcoholic tipsiness begins to wear off, now transforming the guests' demeanor from positivity and joy into irritability and impatience. To give a short speech with a minuscule amount of substance, or to prepare a drawn-out speech—certain to lose the audience's interest—and still omitting necessary details in order to elaborate on the complete essence of Justin and Miranda's character; that was my dilemma. Debating with myself, like an individual lawyer representing two sides of the same case, either path I committed towards would not serve justice. As I rebutted myself from and to myself tirelessly, it was apparent the back and forth was pointless, with my imaginary court adjourning as a lose-lose judgment every single time. The wedding celebration, at the time, was planned for a little under a year ahead in October of 2020, so I knew time was on my side to make a decision. With that being said, the same predicament stared me in the face regardless of how distant the wedding was.

As the direction of my best man speech was yet undecided, I concluded the most advantageous action for me to take was to start making some sort of progress on the speech, so I started creating a brief outline of the topics, stories, and distinctive character traits I planned to discuss. Then, suddenly, out of the ether a quote from Benjamin Franklin flashed into my head, "Either write something worth reading, or do something worth writing about." At that exact moment it became obvious to me what must be done. Justin and Miranda's marriage idea resonated with the latter portion of Franklin's quote. It was my duty to be responsible for the former part. I decided right then and there that instead of writing a verbal address as my best man speech, I would embark on the journey and adventure of writing a book. I arrived at the conclusion that publishing a book in place of the best man speech was the only appropriate act to perform given the special circumstances. Obviously, writing these lines instead of drafting a short speech was the more difficult and time-consuming path to travel, but I knew deep down it was the right thing to do—no matter what adversity and obstacles were to be faced along the way. It would have been a disservice if this piece of literature was not written. A disservice it would have been not only to Justin and Miranda but even more so to myself. It would have been a conscious choice to decline the challenge, completely disregarding everything Justin and Miranda stand for. I was guided to the proposal and it was my choice to say, "I do." However, in reality my journey amounts to a stroll in the park on a warm summer day smiling while eating ice cream compared to the colossal quest Justin and Miranda are choosing to welcome. The wedding, marriage, and character of Justin and Miranda are far from 'cookie cutter,' as we'll explore throughout this book. It makes sense for the best man speech to be no different and reciprocate their courageous spirits accordingly.

As a side note, there are two parts to *The 2650 Mile Aisle*; "Part 1: Pre-Miranda" and "Part 2: Post-Miranda." The majority of the first section—following the introduction—focuses on how Justin came to be the man he is today. Most of this time-period was previous to meeting his soul mate Miranda, who undeniably polished for the better his already sound foundation. The larger portion of "Part 1: Pre-Miranda" will mention Justin. Despite this, a safe assumption can be made that anytime his name is discussed when describing a character trait, Miranda's name can be used interchangeably. The actual event being examined relating to Justin will differ from an event in Miranda's younger days, but I guarantee there is a resemblance in the intrinsic mentality and character.

"Part 2: Post-Miranda" obviously takes place from the time after Justin and Miranda initially met up until the present day. Consider Part 1 and Part 2 separate books, but more comparable to the likes of a series. To grasp either one fully both must be understood. It will be impossible to be receptive of the meaning of Part 2 without the complete understanding of Part 1. Vice versa, the concepts in Part 1 are not complete without the addition of Part 2. The marriage of "Part 1: Pre-Miranda" and "Part 2: Post-Miranda" captures the essence of *The 2650 Mile Aisle* to its highest degree. As we navigate through the passion to live, awareness and beauty of Justin and Miranda, and their relationship, this book is intended to inspire and entertain—through a number of injected anecdotes, in a biography-like fashion (nearing hagiography-like; although more critical and truthful). With the preface complete, let the unorthodox best man speech commence, and let us learn what makes Justin and Miranda so extraordinary while unveiling the source of their fearless disposition.

CAMERON JAMES WILLIAMS

CHAPTER 1: INTRODUCTION

Justin and Miranda at the Bridge

Before delving into and analyzing Justin and Miranda's unique wedding choice, which is the main reason for writing *The 2650 Mile Aisle*, I will first begin by setting the tone with a long-form analogy for this piece of literature. The symbolic meaning will become increasingly clearer with the turn of each page. I am aware that the metaphor to the poem may seem extreme initially, but as Justin and Miranda's true character is revealed and peeled back layer by layer like an onion, the bigger picture will make sense. Although Justin is my brother, my intentions are to remain as unbiased and objective as possible when describing any story or attribute. With that being said, inspiration does in fact touch the emotional chords that exist deep within us. My goal is to pass to you, the reader, the sense of inspiration I receive when I reflect and meditate on Justin and Miranda's conscious excellence. I have concluded the most effective way of doing this is to write straight from the heart and pour my elevated emotional state onto each and every page. Ideally, my objective is to have the reader's feelings regarding Justin and Miranda and their story to correspond and align exactly with my own relative feelings. But even if only a portion of my deep feelings of inspiration and will to live life are reciprocated, I will rest easy at night knowing my job is complete.

Descriptive words can be written, and personal emotions can be discussed, but feelings and experiences are much more sacred. I wish that it was possible to lend my mind, body, and spirit to the audience so that the importance of Justin and Miranda and the meaning behind their endeavors were truly understood. Without a doubt, reading about something invokes a degree of transcendence to an elevated state of mind, yet it's still not comparable to the ascension induced from feeling and experiencing that same thing. I will bridge this gap so that reading transforms into feeling. Plato once said something along the lines of, and I paraphrase:

A painting of a mountain is beautiful but will never be more beautiful than the actual mountain itself. The feelings invoked from looking at the painting will be similar to those of the actual mountain; but never exact. The closer the artist can imitate and express the real mountain, the better he or she is at art.

And to further elaborate on that point, I can read twenty books on how to drive a Lamborghini and study them for years—but until I actually rev the engine when taking one for spin, I will never truly know what the experience feels like. I hope to buckle you up in the driver's seat and get you on the road during and after reading *The 2650 Mile Aisle*.

Now, before we follow Justin and Miranda down their adventurous trail, let us switch gears and shift our focus to the famous poem and mentioned metaphor, *Horatius at the Bridge*. This classic piece of literature was written by Thomas Babington Macaulay in 1842. The memorable ballad recounts the courage of Horatius Cocles in his battle with the Roman army against the Etruscans. The powerful poem consists of nearly six hundred lines, all of which are beautiful, but a condensed version and summaries of the most moving lines that signify the underlying message will be shared. If *Horatius at the Bridge* has already been read, the reinforcement will be beneficial better yet. Macaulay's following lines will be plenty to express the greatness of Horatius (with that being said, I do suggest that the poem be read in its entirety. P.S. it will positively impact your life).

But first, a brief backstory is necessary for a proper and complete understanding. Lars Porsena was the most powerful king in Etruscan Italy, of whom Tarquinius Superbus asked to help him take back Rome. Porsena sent a message to Rome saying they should receive Tarquin as their king, and when the Romans refused, he declared war on them. Horatius Cocles was the keeper of the Gate of Rome. The ballad begins with a description of Lars Porsena:

Lars Porsena of Clusium,
by the Nine Gods he swore
That the great house of Tarquin
Should suffer wrong no more.
By the Nine Gods he swore it, 5
And named a trysting-day,
And bade his messengers ride forth,
East and West and South and North,
To summon his army.

East and West and South and North 10
The messengers ride fast,
And tower and town and cottage
Have heard the trumpet's blast.
Shame on the false Etruscan
Who lingers in his home, 15
When Porsena of Clusium
Is on the march for Rome!

And the poem continues to depict the magnitude of Lars Porsena's reign. At this point he seems invincible as his whole loyal city is behind him.

There be thirty chosen prophets,
The wisest of the land,
Who always by Lars Porsena
Both morn and evening stand.
Evening and morn the Thirty 70
Have turned the verses o'er,
Traced from the right on linen white
By mighty seers of yore;

And with one voice the Thirty
Have their glad answer given: 75
"Go forth, go forth, Lars Porsena, —
Go forth, beloved of Heaven!
Go, and return in glory
To Clusium's royal dome,
And hang round Nurscia's altars
The golden shields of Rome!"

The attack on Rome was now underway. Horatius, keeper of the Gate of Rome, is Consul's nephew.

To eastward and to westward 130
Have spread the Tuscan bands,
Nor house, nor fence, nor dovecote
In Crustumerium stands.
Verbenna down to Ostia
Hath wasted all the plain;
Astur hath stormed Janiculum,
And the stout guards are slain.

I wis, in all the Senate,
There was no heart so bold
But sore it ached, and fast it beat, 140
When that ill news was told.
Forthwith up rose the Consul,
Up rose the Fathers all;
In haste they girded up their gowns,
And hied them to the wall. 145

They held a council, standing
Before the River-Gate;
Short time was there, ye well may guess,
For musing or debate.
Out spake the Consul roundly: 150
"The bridge must straight go down;
For, since Janiculum is lost,
Naught else can save the town."

Just then a scout came flying,
All wild with haste and fear: 155
"To arms! to arms, Sir Consul, —
Lars Porsena is here."

Now, with Janiculum, the last major city before the bridge, destroyed, all hope of saving their homeland was lost. That is, until Horatius steps in.

"Their van will be upon us
Before the bridge goes down;
And if they once may win the bridge, 215
What hope to save the town?"

Then out spoke Horatius,
The Captain of the gate;
"To every man upon this earth
Death cometh soon or late. 220
And how can man die better
Than facing fearful odds
For the ashes of his fathers
And the temples of his Gods,

And for the tender mother
Who dandled him to rest,
And for the wife who nurses
His baby at her breast,
And for the holy maidens
Who feed the eternal flame, —
To save them from false Sextus
That wrought the deed of shame?"

Horatius continues his monumental proclamation...

"Hew down the bridge, Sir Consul,
With all the speed ye may;
I, with two or more to help me,
Will hold the foe in play.
In yon straight path a thousand
May well be stopped by three:
Now who will stand on either hand,
And keep the bridge with me?"

Two fearless souls joined Horatius in defense of warding off the Etruscans. Then out spoke the Consul.

"Horatius," quoth the Consul,
"As thou sayest so let it be"'
And straight against that great array
Went forth the dauntless three.

By defending the narrow end of the bridge—Horatius along with two others—were able to hold off the invading army long enough, thus buying time for the other Romans to destroy the bridge behind them. The collapsing of the bridge blocked the Etruscans' attack and saved the city. The final lines of *Horatius at the Bridge* are a fitting closure and embody Horatius' immortal spirit elegantly:

> *With weeping and with laughter*
> *Still is the story told,*
> *How well Horatius kept the bridge*
> *In the brave days of the old.*[1] 589

The sacrifice of Horatius at the bridge was quite honorable and admirable to say the least. While against all odds, his courage and boldness to pursue greatness in his magnificent act of stepping outside the norm is a timeless theme that reoccurs throughout history and still proves true in current times. The reason *Horatius at the Bridge* was chosen to set the tone for us is because the inspiration received after reading the poem harmonizes with the emotional chords plucked and inspiration ignited deep within when contemplating and reflecting on Justin and Miranda's story. Going 'against the grain' is a risk, and certainly a leap of faith into the unknown, but the potential reward for doing so is a merit worthy of the highest honor. The late co-founder of Apple Inc., Steve Jobs, who dropped out of Harvard to pursue his goal with

Steve Wozniak, started a now multi-billion-dollar company in Jobs' garage. Their venture exemplifies this theme precisely. If the Founding Fathers were alive today, I'm sure they would agree as well that pure brilliance and greatness in life does not arise from being 'normal.' If they hadn't unlocked the courageous power that lived deep within them, who knows what the United States of America would look like today? If John Hancock never executed his famous signature, would Great Britain still be ruling the colonies? If a resilient group of young men never dumped tea into the Boston Harbor, would the King of England be in control today? The point is nothing truly notable ever came from following the herd. With great certitude, it is a proven fact that the leap of faith into the unknown is where unmanifested brilliance rests.

As Ralph Waldo Emerson, the American philosopher, essayist, poet and leader of the transcendentalist movement in the mid-nineteenth century famously proclaimed in his essay *Self-Reliance*:

> "Pythagoras was misunderstood, and Socrates, and Jesus, and Luther, and Copernicus, and Galileo, and Newton, and every pure and wise spirit that ever took flesh. To be great is to be misunderstood."[2]

Now, certainly, there are varying degrees of greatness—and I am not saying Justin and Miranda are comparable to Jesus or Socrates—but greatness is, in fact, greatness no matter the magnitude.

Throughout this book, we will discover what drives individuals to go above and beyond a mundane lifestyle. Also, I will impart where the source of that character trait spans from, and how it becomes manifested into a human being. I will explore what exactly makes Justin and Miranda worthy to be mentioned in the discussion of greatness. After learning about the magnificent feat these two are setting out to accomplish, I think you'll agree as well.

The Announcement

Let us take time this section to bring to the surface Justin and Miranda's wedding plan announcement, which is the main reason for writing *The 2650 Mile Aisle*. Right now, we are not so much concerned about the time and place of the announcement, as the sequence of events would be jumbled, ultimately causing confusion (later on, the setting will be explored and explained further when fitting properly into chronological order). Nonetheless, it is necessary to set the mood and describe the scene. More so than the actual act of announcing, the substance of Justin and Miranda's announcement is what captures the true meaning and deeper essence at hand.

Last summer, in July of 2019—Justin and Miranda, already engaged at the time—the Williams family plus Miranda traveled all the way across the country for a vacation to California. Born and raised in Pittsburgh, no one in my immediate family had previously ventured westward enough in the United States to experience the Pacific Ocean first-hand. My older sister, Alexa is a year younger than Justin and three older than me. She is a nurse who loves to travel and laugh, but the farthest west she previously traveled was Colorado. Abbey, my younger sister, is four years younger than me and arguably the funniest Williams in the family. The closest she journeyed to the Pacific Ocean was

Colorado as well. Justin is the oldest sibling and substantially the tallest Williams, but trust me, we will learn plenty about him soon (alright, I swear my parents maxed out at four kids). Our dad, also known as Papa Bear or Diddy, is the financial controller for a company that specializes in pharmaceutical tablet presses. In our dad's younger days, his involvement in submission wrestling led him out to Las Vegas for a competition, however, he still hadn't reached the Pacific. It is safe to say his witty sense of humor was passed down to all my siblings. Our mom, who is exceedingly clever in her own right, did not join the westward trip since she resides in Florida. Miranda, growing up in Colorado—although not as distant to California as the Williams family—had not made her way to the Pacific seashore either as there were numerous outdoor activities to occupy her time living as close to the Rocky Mountains as she did. Her and Justin's most westward location set foot upon was Arizona, as they had recently explored the Grand Canyon.

  It was a week of firsts for everybody. I viewed the trip as an official acceptance and welcoming of Miranda to the Williams family, as Justin had 'popped the question' to Miranda nine months prior on a four-day-long backpacking trip in Arizona. Unlike a conventional vacation to a condo or resort on the beach—laying around, forgetting to apply sunscreen, and stuffing our faces with seafood—we approached this trip differently (although I still did get sunburn). We divided the trip into three parts, each in a distinct location along the coast. Justin and Miranda created an action-packed itinerary for the week out west, full of early morning hikes (one of which was ten miles), and plenty of sight-seeing, among other outdoor activities. It was a week filled to the brim with adventure, and when thinking back on it, the excitement made it one of the most enjoyable vacations to date.

Upon arriving in San Francisco the first day, we unpacked and settled into the Airbnb we would be sleeping in for the next two nights. It was around 3 o'clock, so after fueling up at a local coffee shop, we set out for the city to explore it. Justin and Miranda treated the quest through San Francisco as sacred, as they treated any experience grand or not the same. After navigating through Chinatown, and looking at Alcatraz Island in awe, it was dinnertime. Together, we perched up by the Bay and enjoyed the freshest helpings of clam chowder that I have gobbled down hitherto. The chowder was served in a mountainous bread bowl that absorbed the delicious seafood juices (I am salivating just thinking about it).

While Abbey and I were soaking in the gorgeous view and sunshine, like a sponge absorbing water through every pore (or like the bread bowl and the chowder), we overheard Justin and Miranda whispering to each other about something. Being 'Nebby Nellies,' all we were able to piece together from the conversation were the words *announcement* and *later on tonight*. The rest of dinner and the evening turned into a discreet guessing game, as Justin and Miranda weren't aware of our clue. Alexa, Abbey, my dad, and I tossed out ideas of what the reason was for the secretive big announcement. Everyone's initial inclination was that Miranda must have been pregnant. With Justin and Miranda becoming engaged relatively shortly before then, and the wedding date planned for over a year in the future, it was the only logical guess. I was going to be an uncle for the first time! My sisters would soon accept the role of aunt seriously and our parents would have their first grandchild. Our guessing game turned into what they would name their child. And then Abbey pointed out that Miranda was unwinding from the long day of travel with an ice-cold beer, so that idea was shot down. In our exclusive brainstorm-session we all took a stab at guessing what the purpose of the announcement later that night would entail.

"They are moving to Colorado from Michigan," my dad proposed.

"Justin is finally selling his 1998 Honda Civic," Alexa said, with the rest of us responding with a chuckle.

"Miranda is calling off the wedding," I announced sarcastically, all of us laughing together as our family always had something witty to say amongst or towards each other. But no matter what was ever said we knew it was all in love. The idea pitching then turned into a joke session as we really had no idea what the announcement was related to. It seemed to turn into a contest of who could think of the most off-the-wall idea at that point. But in all seriousness, the suspense was building up in us. Looking back now, our exaggerated guesses weren't all too far from the truth, believe it or not, although completely not in the manner expected. After scarfing down the last pieces of the bread bowl—the Williams family and Miranda watched the sun sink into the water—gazing off into the colorful horizon at the breathtaking view. Then we gathered our belongings and hurried to the rental car. The twenty-minute drive returning back to the house felt like a millennium. Feeling like a bunch of kids the night before Christmas eager to open the presents Santa Claus brought them the next morning, we were excited to finally learn what Justin and Miranda were going to announce to us.

    Alas, we arrived at our bunker. Wasting no time Justin and Miranda gathered us in the living room and revealed they had an announcement to make. Acting surprised on the surface, while underneath overflowing with excitement, we scampered to congregate. My sisters claimed the couch, my dad sunk into the loveseat, and I occupied the bench at the table. Justin and Miranda assembled front and center, standing in front of the fireplace—now with everybody's undivided attention.

"I'm going to be an uncle!" I stood up with my arms raised victoriously above my head. My brother and soon to be sister-in-law couldn't help but laugh, even though I now sensed a serious look in their eyes. They both took a deep breath simultaneously, with the room silent enough to hear a pin drop.

The lovers began their announcement with Justin taking the lead, "So as we all know, the wedding is planned for next year." My sisters, dad, and I glanced over at each other wondering what he would say next. "We are going to celebrate our marriage, but Miranda and I have chosen to do things differently. Instead of spending money on a traditional wedding like we originally thought, we are going to quit our jobs for six months and use that money to hike the Pacific Crest Trail. Once our adventure is complete, we will go back to Miranda's house in Colorado to celebrate. The celebration will be significantly downsized compared to a conventional wedding, but we are still going to invite immediate family and friends. We will then start our lives together in Colorado." In shock, still piecing together what he just said (I mind you that a few years prior Justin and Miranda had settled in Michigan into well-paying jobs as an engineer and dietitian, respectively), the questions started to fire at him like a machine gun, as my family and I were trying to gain an understanding of what all of that meant.

"What's the Pacific Crest Trail?"

"Wait, what do you mean?"

"When are you guys doing this?"

"What about the wedding?" We bombarded them to help grasp what the announcement meant.

Miranda answered the first inquiry to start, "The Pacific Crest Trail is a trail that starts in New Mexico and extends all the way up to the tip of Washington. It is a 2650-mile hike so we need to start in March in order to have time to finish the trail before the end of summer. This is something we really want to do, and the time is now or never. It will be unrealistic to make this type of commitment once life gets going and we have children, starting our own family. Like Justin said, we are going to start our lives fresh and officially move out to Colorado after the celebration in October."

Justin piggybacked on her thought, "We will find jobs in Colorado afterward and end up buying a house out there."

My family is thoughtful, intelligent, and open-minded. No matter what choices any of us make in life, assuming there is no harm involved, we always support each other. With that being said, I sensed my family members' moods shift immediately from joy and freedom to a state of confusion. I could feel some sort of void in the atmosphere. Everybody genuinely congratulated the both of them, almost hesitantly, still continuing to inquire about the hike and change of plans as if they were missing an important piece of the puzzle, trying to make sense of what was just said. Granted, from a conservative view, there was not a single answer that could be given to cushion the uncertainty and risk of quitting steady jobs and comfortable lifestyle to travel off the grid into the wilderness for six months. The same questions were rephrased a few times to confirm the understanding was correct; it was. The unconventional approach, as to be expected, was difficult for everyone to grasp entirely. I, on a different hand—although initially shocked until having a few minutes to digest their plan, yet still not grasping it wholly—sat on the bench uncontrollably gratified by them. I felt a rush of inspiration deep within and a subtle weight lifted off my shoulders. I admire a courageous soul, and the motive underneath Justin and Miranda's announcement embodied that type of spirit completely. The conscious decision to hike into the unknown for six months is without a doubt bold—but I realized that if Justin and Miranda arrived at this choice it was well thought out—and unquestionably precisely planned.

My brother said to me later on when addressing the risk of finding a new job in Colorado that he was sure he would land a position somewhere. He first made the point of how his engineering degree would certainly increase his chances. And then he made another valid point. He added that there would be no better interview

THE 2650 MILE AISLE

response when the hiring manager asks him to, "Think of a time when you had to face adversity to accomplish your goals." "Yeah, over six months ago I left my well-paying job to hike 2650 miles along the West Coast," he said nonchalantly, with the utmost confidence he would find another secure job.

On the surface—without a question—the act of hiking up the entire coast seems crazy, but the underlying meaning and intention of the act penetrates more deeply below the superficial surface. What's more special than finishing this hike is the act of consciously embarking on the journey. The underlying meaning and intention are the truly important and admirable aspects from my perspective. One can draw a comparison of Justin and Miranda and their choice of hiking to an iceberg: The tip above the surface of the water is just a small glimpse of the massive piece of ice in its entirety. The majority of the substance is actually underneath what is visible to the eye. But when the lens and angle are changed slightly, there lies the whole iceberg.

The act of hiking is simply an epitome or microcosm of the character, spirit and life force that exists below the surface of Justin and Miranda. The Pacific Crest Trail is a particular instance that expresses and illustrates a more general way of living. "To see greatness, one must in fact be great" is an expression from an unknown source. Another way of saying this would be "Like recognize like."

With respect to Justin and Miranda, one must actively match their state of consciousness to comprehend them and their choice properly. A separation from trivial and material matters is a great first step. For example, the human eye is simply a bundle of nerves that reflect light. With that being said, the function of the eye producing sight is rather astonishing when viewed properly and in its full capacity. The function, which cannot be seen or interpreted at the surface is what makes the eyeball—and Justin and Miranda—so incredibly meaningful and immensely beautiful.

Justin and Miranda's quest is into the wilderness—and my quest is to discover the source of this type of character; as well as the driving power that opens a portal into elevated realms, enabling an individual to go above and beyond the 'normal' way of life. Justin and Miranda possess the ability to access this portal to a transcended and beautiful place, which every human being is capable, more simply and often than the average person. Yes, I am positive that there is some degree of pain and suffering in their everyday lives, as we all go through stints of this drudgery, but certainly they hold the knowledge to limit it through their sense of being and way of living. Optimistically, learning about Justin and Miranda will give us insight on how to unlock this latent power of peace and presence that exists in all of us. Wayne Dyer, a self-help author and motivational speaker once stated, "If you change the way you look at things, the things you look at change."[1] It matters not if this perspective on life was learned by Justin and Miranda or if it is innately engrained in human beings, simply there to be realized—but I am certain that the both of them understand the meaning of this quote flawlessly. Now, for us to understand the full implications of their journey into the wild, we must first learn about the Pacific Crest Trail.

CAMERON JAMES WILLIAMS

The Pacific Crest Trail

The Pacific Crest Trail is one of only three major trails in the United States that extends from the southernmost border (Mexico) to the northernmost boundary (Canada). The Appalachian Trail and Continental Divide Trail are the other two trails, occupying the eastern and central portion of the United States, respectively. The Appalachian Trail runs from Georgia all the way up to Maine, while the Continental Divide Trail stretches from New Mexico to Montana. But we are not here for a geography lesson. That said, the Pacific Crest Trail Justin and Miranda are hiking traverses the western portion of the United States, spanning from the southern tip of California up to the US-Canada border. It is a treasured pathway through some of the most outstanding scenic terrain in the United States—from scorching deserts to snow-capped mountains. Being America's second-longest trail at 2650-miles long, the trek's Southern Terminus is located in Campo, California, a small town on the US-Mexico border—and the trail passes through California, Oregon, and Washington before reaching the Northern Terminus at the US-Canada border in Manning Park, British Columbia.[1] Most folks leisurely hike only a portion of one or two of the Pacific Crest Trail's thirty sections. With each section averaging eleven miles, they divide throughout the coast as follows: eighteen sections in California; seven in Oregon; and five in Washington. But why not hike them all at once?

The more experienced hikers (or those balancing lack of experience with fearlessness) who slog the entire path do so with only a backpack filled with bare necessities in something commonly called a thru-hike. The definition of a thru-hike is to long-distance hike from end-to-end, in Justin and Miranda's case from Campo to Manning Park. Those who thru-hike carry minimal supplies for survival in their backpacks—food, water, limited equipment, and shelter. A one-person tent, hardly able to fit in the backpack, is the shelter for a backpacking trip. One could classify Justin and Miranda as seasoned hikers, having backpacked throughout different areas of Michigan and enduring a four-day excursion in the Grand Canyon—but those experiences will prove to be a drop in the bucket compared to the vastness of the 2650 miles of the Pacific Crest Trail. Rather than a four-day episode, their journey this time will be a 4-6 month ordeal. Individuals hiking the Pacific Crest Trail must leave early enough in the spring to not get boiled in the desert's summer sun. Also, if the departure is too early, the snow accumulation in the Sierra Nevada from the previous winter—due to its increased elevation and low temperatures—will not receive ample time and temperature increase to melt. On the contrary, if starting too late, treacherous winter weather up

North will halt the excursion come fall. The factors involved in both leaving too early or too late must be calculated and balanced accordingly. Usually, adventurers begin their pilgrimage precisely in March or April and finish around August or September. For the footslog of the Pacific Crest Trail to be completed in its entirety within this timeframe, 10-20 miles per day on average must be hiked.

     Obviously, it is impossible to carry six months of food and equipment in a backpack all at once. Consequently, it is imperative for anyone who decides to press their luck and test their skills against the behemoth of a trail that an orchestrated resupply strategy is in place. Normally, no more than ten days of food is carried at one time. Anything additional to that physically taxes the thru-hiker with an unnecessary burden, while anything less than ten days is also burdensome for the individuals in a different sense, needing to resupply more frequently.

     Throughout the endeavor, all four seasons will be experienced—ranging from overwhelming heat and sunshine to blistering frigid temperatures. Because of this, resupply boxes of food, gear, and clothing (based on the predicted conditions of the studied terrain) need to be mailed via USPS to resupply stations in towns along the way. For instance, sunblock may be critical in the Mojave Desert; while ice axes are vital in the Sierra Nevada since Justin and Miranda plan to summit Mount

THE 2650 MILE AISLE

Whitney—the tallest mountain in the contiguous United States. Also, lightweight hiking shoes—and any pair of shoes for that matter—become worn out after roughly 400 miles, perhaps less considering the uneven terrain on the trail. Because of this, approximately five to six pairs of shoes will be needed throughout the entire trek, and obviously, not every pair is carried at once. All the resupply packages can be shipped out prior to the hike, but it is increasingly more expensive that way. Instead, most people pack all the boxes beforehand and rely on someone to ship them to each checkpoint at the mutually agreed upon designated time throughout the trip. Every ounce of nutrient-dense, high-calorie food bundled in the packages is strategically selected. Common fuel enjoyed in transit are: dried fruits, nuts, peanut butter, crackers, protein bars, and beef jerky—to name a few items.

Water, on the other hand, is an entirely different story along the trail. For the most part Justin and Miranda will hydrate via streams throughout their quest. With that being said, at some points hikers are faced with 25-30 miles stretches before they reach water. The water shortage is especially true in parts of the desert and also some portions of Northern California. There is hardly any room for error in this regard as human beings potentially risk dehydration within three days of not drinking water. When plodding up to twenty miles a day—burning calories more rapidly and sweating often—that timeframe is reduced even further. Meticulously planning ahead with an adequate resupply strategy, taking into account food, water, and equipment, is by no means a trivial task prior to reaching the Southern Terminus of the Pacific Crest Trail. With that being said, more than just a stellar resupply strategy is required for success on the journey. First and foremost, a permit to even begin to hike the trail needs to be obtained.

    For courageous souls hiking 500 or more continuous miles, a thru-hiking permit is required. The U.S. Forest Service authorizes the Pacific Crest Trail Association (PCTA) to issue these permits in order to preserve the natural habitat of the terrain as well as for hiker safety. Permits are free but are distributed on a first-come, first-served basis.[2] Individuals who apply for the permit are in no way, shape, or form guaranteed to receive it. Each adult must secure his/her own permit, so both Justin and Miranda are obligated to show proof of a permit in order to gain access to the Pacific Crest Trail. I will revisit the following point more thoroughly later on, but Justin and Miranda were 100% set on their trip before the permits were even reviewed and administered. Each of them is exceedingly sure in themselves in any task they approach, and the permits proved to be no different. They weren't as confident in the thing they couldn't control—the actual review process—but were certain they would hike the Pacific Crest Trail one way or another if it was the last thing they did. Whether pushing their planned start date back, forward, or capitalizing on a forfeited permit, they made their decision and there was no turning back. To their fortune, there were not any troubles receiving the permits on the first attempt.

Annually, a high percentage of permit holders don't follow through with their trip plans (surprisingly, or maybe not so much). Due to changing life circumstances, motivations or injuries, many people change their minds about the trail. Fortunately for Justin and Miranda, the permit process went smoothly as they intentionally picked an unpopular start date. In addition to the thru-hike permit, a California Fire Permit is also essential. As wildfires in California happen in high frequencies, the permit mitigates the risk of a hiker starting a forest fire.[3] When traveling through California on a thru-hike, obtaining the California Fire Permit is critical for primarily two reasons. First off, and arguably more important, when a water filtration device is unavailable, fires are created to boil water, purifying it and killing any diseases or bacteria present in stream water. Precautionary measures like those just mentioned help to prevent sickness during the expedition. Secondly, and still very important, fire will cook any foods that are unable to be eaten raw. In addition to the required California Fire Permit, there are still designated areas in California where permit holders are allowed to have a fire. Believe it or not, permits and resupply strategies are not the only concerns for hikers encountering the Pacific

Crest Trail. Inherent in the trail is an abundance of risks and dangers.

The PCTA estimates only 700-800 people attempt the complete route each year. Of these 700-800, only about 60% of them finish what they started.[4] Dangers characteristic of the Pacific Crest Trail are bears, mountain lions, bees in Northern California, and rattlesnakes. Strangely enough, wild animals prove to be the least of a hiker's worries. Statistics show lightning strikes, drowning, falls, poisonous plants, disease, and heatstroke pose a greater threat. Valley fever, for instance, is a horrific lung infection caused from a fungus that lives in the soil throughout the Southwest. The Pacific Crest Trail likely passes through areas where this fungus exists.[5] Giardia, a microscopic parasite, is also potentially troubling to even the most experienced hikers. The symptoms of the parasite are diarrhea, flatulence, greasy stools that float, abdominal cramps, upset stomach, and nausea.[6] Giardia can put a damper on anybody's journey and perhaps bring it to a screeching halt. Some plants found on the Pacific Crest Trail are debatably more dangerous than the animals. One of these poisonous plants, which lives in Southern California, is the poodle-dog bush.[7] In appearance and smell, this plant is extremely similar to the cannabis plant. But if smoked, the next stop will be the hospital for the uninformed individual. Even if touched, the poodle-dog bush induces an unbearable rash similar to the poison oak plant, which is another troublesome plant along the way. In Northern California, the poison oak plant proves to be vexatious. At times it is easy to avoid, but sometimes unavoidable dense stretches of the poison oak continue for miles at a time. The symptoms impose a hamper on the adventure through the wilderness. In addition to diseases and plants, stream crossing constitutes a hazard for hikers. First of all, getting swept by the current and drowning in the rapids is a legitimate risk. And less apparent, hypothermia caused by the freezing water from the melting snow runoff of the previous winter is also an issue of concern.

    The total number of deaths on the Pacific Crest Trail is not documented, but at least seventeen deaths have been recorded.[8] One of the individuals who confronted this unfortunate fate was John Lowder, a doctor from San Diego. In June of 1999, John slipped on ice while crossing the New Army Pass in the Sierra, resulting in broken bones and a head injury. He was found in a sleeping bag by rescuers following the incident. Unfortunately, they didn't make it in time to save John.[9] The adventure on the Pacific Crest Trail also ended less than desirable, to say the least, for Timothy Evan Nodol. In 2014, Timothy began to feel sick and reached out to emergency services. Firefighters eventually reached him and carried out their procedural tests of symptoms. Shortly after, he went into arrest and the team was unable to resuscitate him.[10] Another brave—yet unfortunate—soul was Wang Chaocui, who was discovered in a river in the Kerrick Canyon located in the Yosemite National Park.[11] 2017 was a freakishly dangerous year to hike the Pacific Crest Trail because of the treacherous snowfall the winter prior. River crossings especially posed a high degree of risk for hikers that year.

The bodies of the mentioned individuals may have passed but their fearless spirit lives on in those woods for eternity. To prove this, year after year, people from around the world continue to gravitate to the Pacific Crest Trail to be a part of something bigger than themselves. Despite the hapless fates of the hikers mentioned, it is not common to die on the trail. Regardless, in the wild, there is no telling the unseen obstacles, challenges, risks, and dangers one may face. Although not everyone makes it out alive, for those fortunate enough the reward is an astonishing and life-changing experience. The most notable of these experiences is Cheryl Strayed's exploit, which is documented and described in her book *Wild: From Lost to Found*. The book, reaching #1 on the New York Times Best Seller list, is a memoir of her 2012 journey. *Wild: From Lost to Found* was also a first selection for Oprah's Book Club 2.0. As Amazon's product description of the #1 Bestseller states:

At 21, Cheryl Strayed thought she had lost everything, in the wake of her mother's death, her family scattered and her own marriage was destroyed. Four years later, with nothing to lose, she made the most impulsive decision of her life. With no experience or training, driven only by blind will, she would hike more than 1000 miles of the Pacific Crest Trail from the Mojave Desert through California and Oregon to Washington State—and would do it alone. Told with suspense and style, sparkling with warmth and humor Wild powerfully captures the terrors and pleasures of one young woman forging ahead against all odds on a journey that maddened, strengthened, and ultimately healed her.[12]

Now that we are familiarized with the ins-and-outs of the Pacific Crest Trail—learning what it is, how one goes about hiking it, and risks involved, among other things—we may take the next step in our own journey. We shall continue our quest to unveil what makes two individuals willingly want to cut all ties and not turn back—just as Horatius had done at the bridge—and dive head-first into unknown territory and the uncertain outcome of the Pacific Crest Trail.

CAMERON JAMES WILLIAMS

PART 1: PRE-MIRANDA

CAMERON JAMES WILLIAMS

Part 1: Pre-Miranda

Where It All Started

In Part 1, we will enter a time portal and travel back in time to where *it* all started for Justin. I have already briefly mentioned what 'it' is referring to, so I will not delve too much deeper into that aspect directly. To reemphasize, *it* is what makes Justin fearlessly strive to go above and beyond whatever task is at hand. *It* is what enables Justin to have the courage to stand alone. *It* is an indescribable place at its roots—but surely one of peace and presence. The character of an individual is built up over time. It is like building a house—as it starts with a solid foundation and then bricks are precisely laid on top of each other one at a time—increasingly solidifying the structure. Bo Schembechler, a legendary football coach at Michigan, once said, "Every day you either improve or you get worse. You never stay the same".[1] That quote speaks volumes in respect to character. It is a conscious decision made every moment of every day. Character is what truly differentiates us all as human beings. Throughout

Part 1, we will take a first-hand look at the constructed foundation and bricks laid that ultimately lead to Justin's current analogous house—which is still a work in progress—as I am sure Justin would demand that to be said.

    Miranda won't be mentioned in this section as it would not be appropriate according to the timeline of the text and reality. She will be given a warm and thorough welcoming in "Part 2: Post-Miranda." With that being said, it is absolutely necessary to note again that anytime Justin and his character is mentioned in Part 1, feel free to substitute Miranda's name. I reemphasize this not because the specific acts or things she has accomplished are remotely similar, but because the causal general principle—resulting in the things achieved—can be matched nearly identically. The underlying principles, morals, and intentions of both Justin and Miranda's characters mirror each other closely. Although arriving to each other from two vastly different cultures and childhoods—what makes Justin, Justin and what makes Miranda, Miranda—are eerily similar. As we will learn later on in Part 2, they truly are two peas in a pod. As Justin's brother, it should come to no surprise that I know a great deal of intricate details about his younger years, observing and learning how he developed into the individual he is today. My brief, entry-level knowledge of Miranda's youth is merely a seminar compared to the masters degree I have received in Justin's past. It is one thing to have heard stories about someone, and yet a whole different delineation to have experienced and witnessed somebody firsthand, as I have with my older brother.

CAMERON JAMES WILLIAMS

CHAPTER 2: RESPECT IS EARNED; NOT GIVEN

Meaning of an Older Brother

The age-old saying "Blood is thicker than water" certainly rings true for most people to at least some degree. For me personally, my family is everything. Literally none of us would be here if it wasn't for family. Furthermore, family members are the ones that no matter how tough the going gets, they are there. And when push comes to shove, no matter what previous arguments arose, or misunderstandings surfaced, family is there to support each other once again. Part of this is because of the tribal instinct from thousands of years ago still remaining in us humans from our evolutionary past. It was a life or death situation for us when it came down to battling another tribe or group to protect ourselves and our kin—to survive. No individual, especially long ago, was able to survive on his/her own. Another group would swoop in and demolish the individual and his/her resources with ease. Because of this, a tight-knit family that evolved to survive was critical.

Nowadays, family is not as much required for survival in its most barbaric form, but certainly still serves a purpose for support, love, and fitness within society. Families transpire in all sorts of shapes and sizes, but in any case, DNA is shared amongst the members which is astonishing in its own right.

Mothers, through the miracle of birth and glorious sacrifice, bring us all into this world. Fathers, on the other hand, play just as an important role in contributing to the alchemy of creation—although not as physically strenuous. Mothers and fathers nurture, care, and teach us how to live on our own in this world. A daunting task, but one that is always performed so graciously by parents. For these reasons, among others, there is and always will be a special connection between a parent and child. Another potent relationship in a family is that of a grandparent and a grandchild. Although not always as closely bonded compared to a parent and child, in this significant relationship, there is no shortage of love and affection between the family members. Moreover, in certain cases a grandparent steps in and plays the role of a parent flawlessly. The connection between siblings is as unique and powerful as any other relationship within a family. Arguably, in some instances the consanguinity amongst siblings is stronger than any other relationship within the family tree.

THE 2650 MILE AISLE

And for the readers with a brother(s), I think we can all agree that the brother to brother connection is perhaps the strongest. The bond between brothers is one that cannot be broken. A brother is a right-hand man. A brother—although at times perhaps seeming like a worst enemy—is indisputably a best friend. A brother is one of the first people that a laugh is shared with. Conversely, a brother may be the first person to make you cry. But ask anybody with a brother; it is all in love. An older brother takes this meaning to an elevated degree. An older brother teaches the first swear word. An older brother shows how to play kickball for the first time. An older brother may help you get out of trouble the one day and then fart in your face the next. But most importantly, an older brother is a symbol; an image; a role model. An older brother is a guardian; a watchful protector; a leader by example.

  Growing older, I realize how fortunate I am to have Justin as my older brother. He truly embodies the essence of the word in its purest form. Justin has always been a guardian, a protector, when my parents or I couldn't protect myself. Although Justin would more than likely claim this role as being his duty, with him having a tendency of refraining from submitting to his emotional chords. Writing this section gives me a beautiful chance to reflect and reminisce on our time together on this earth thus far. With Justin and I being four years apart, at times when we were younger—due to the maturity gap—it may have been difficult to grasp each other fully. For instance, when he was taking his driver's test, I was taking a spelling test. With that being said, I can't recall a time when our age gap was ever a barrier to understanding each other. As both of us have arrived at full maturity for quite some time now, any possibility of a communication impediment has disintegrated into the ether. While both of us share an appreciation for the intellect as well as a raunchy joke, our conversations are now more enjoyable and insightful than ever. Whether it's dissecting the economy or impersonating somebody from the television screen, a positive takeaway is always the result when Justin is in the equation.

But please don't get me wrong, as civil as we are now, there were a multitude of battles (possibly wars) in our younger days. We will just pan it off as 'boys being boys' looking back on it today, though, as love and brotherhood were always present (although sometimes needing a microscope to see). One of these maybe not so loving recollections is when our family was enjoying an annual family camping trip many years ago.

Being the active crew we were and still are, most of our time was occupied at the camp playground and volleyball court. One night, since the court was inhabited by fellow campers in the midst of a serious match, we utilized our time

THE 2650 MILE AISLE

efficiently. Instead of waiting on the side of the court to join the next game, we constructed our own version and rules of a soccer game. Using the volleyball, the openings between two large oak trees as the net, and pairs of flip-flops as the sidelines—it was game-time. Hours passed, and the volleyball court was now available, but my parents, brother, and sisters continued our makeshift soccer game anyways. Due to our competitive nature, the family was now divided for these couple of hours. The other team (and other half of the family) were now the enemies. Justin, per usual, pushed the limits and towed the line of the created rules, although he would never cross the line. His famous line was and still is, "If you're cheating, you're trying." I never understood what he meant by this until recently, because being the honest guy he is, he would never cheat. Perhaps a more accurate way to phrase this, although myself not realizing it at the time, is, "I am going to do whatever it takes within moral and virtuous guidelines to achieve my goal." In this case it was to win the soccer game that July 4th weekend.

    If he was on your team you loved him, but if not, you hated him. For instance, one time he booted the volleyball a great distance over the goaltender's (my dad) head, yet it was still between the trees. Justin's reaction of jubilation was as if he had just netted a goal for his team. My team looked around puzzled as all the goals scored prior were netted by kicking the ball on or near the ground.

Justin pointed out that the rules created had not specified the height of the top of the goal, and it was a point as long as the ball passed between the large oaks. He was 100% correct, and even though dissatisfied, there was not much my team and I could do. With that being said, immediately following that goal new rules relating to the goal size were implemented. But Justin's previous goal still counted—and rightly so. Occasions like these are when Justin's five-word phrase was iterated.

Shortly after the goal, there was a discrepancy between Justin and me. I can't recall exactly the reason for the dispute, but I vividly remember what happened afterwards. For whatever reason, I hatched the brilliant idea to spit a loogie on my brother. I promptly regretted my decision, and as there was a split-second pause, I remember steam pouring out of my brother's ears and blood shooting out of his eyes (alright maybe I am exaggerating)—and then the hunt was on. Barefooted, the match came to a halt as my brother chased me around the playing field and playground. I bolted around the one oak tree and over the volleyball court, wishfully hoping sand would somehow end up in my brother's eyes to slow him down. This was not the case, as he continued in hot pursuit as I zigged and zagged around the swing set. It was the beginning of dusk, so I tried to convince myself that if it became dark enough I could hide away in the bushes with the groundhogs for the evening. Ultimately, in the back of my mind, I was aware of the inevitably of Justin catching me eventually—because if I darted around that playground all night—surely, he would follow. I felt like a young mouse attempting to scurry from a hungry cat.

My thirteen-year-old lungs were unable to sustain any more sprinting and I lost a step. This gave tenacious Justin the ability to gain ground and catch me. As he finally seized me, I curled up in a fetal position for protection. To my demise, this was no use. In a herculean manner, he hoisted me above his head. For a split second my life flashed before my eyes. It felt like the Simba birth scene from Disney's *Lion King* where Rafiki raises Simba above his head on the edge of the cliff (cue Elton John's "Circle of Life"). Except in this parody, there was not a happy ending for Simba. I was barbarically thwarted to the ground as I said goodbye to the world. Laying there motionless while crying, I knew my punishment was complete. The professional wrestling-style body slam was borderline egregious to say the least, but it was certainly warranted. I can promise you that I have never spit on him since.

Ironically, we were making each other s'mores by the campfire two hours later. Justin is always in competition—not with others—but with himself. For example, although he tried to make the next s'more better than the treat engineered prior, he was still content with the one he had in front of him. The balance between striving for more and enjoying the present moment is beautifully evident when observing Justin. I mind you that less-than-desirable instances like the camping trip escapade happened few and far between, but as the younger brother I am, I couldn't let Justin off the hook too easily and not mention it here.

Switching gears to another memory from our childhood was a weekly ritual of sorts we used to partake in. I believe Justin and I were still seventeen and thirteen, respectively, at the time. Once again, this weekly formal occurrence was completely manufactured from our imaginations—of which there was never a shortage of creative juices flowing. To set the stage, Justin and I shared a room growing up. His bed was on the one side of the room while mine was along the opposite wall. Before we fell asleep, while lying in bed in darkness, each of us would crack jokes back and forth to each other. We giggled and then sternly declared that was the last jest of the evening. Seconds or minutes later something else humorous would be uttered by one of us, both of us blurting out with laughter. Then for some odd but hilarious reason, we upped the ante and created a nightly game that corresponded with each day to battle against each other. 'Moon Man Monday,' 'Ball Tap Tuesday,' 'Wet Willie Wednesday' were some of the dubbed days, probably better off that I have forgotten the names for the other days of the week. For 'Moon Man Monday,' rather than cracking jokes until we fell asleep, we would do things differently on those days. As the name suggests we tried to moon each other before the other person could notice and defend himself accordingly. Mooning, for those who do not know, is the act of showing one's bare buttocks. In this case, we took this concept to the extreme, attempting to place our bare cheeks onto the other's face (looking back this was tremendously unsanitary and rather strange). At any rate, that's how Monday nights played out for quite some time. As with every other activity engaged in with Justin, he was confident he would come out on top—in this case giving the last moon of the evening as I was falling asleep. I still sometimes look back and chuckle (and get the jeebie weebies) on Monday nights before going to sleep. I will save you all the repulsion by not describing the games played during other nights of the week. (Side note: I hope I am able to have children after those stretches of Tuesday nights). Fortunately, for our well-being, we grew out of that phase of our lives after many grueling months. With that being said, many lessons were indirectly taught from our game played, such as: "The best defense is a good offense" and "Always remain vigilant."

Regardless of the few occurrences where we battled each other in our childhoods—now looking back at all the trivial things we did to each other—I can assure you it was all in love. When push came to shove, Justin was always on my team and continues to be today. Being young, we were still figuring things out. Our competitive natures amongst ourselves intensified the fact that when someone wins, somebody else loses. We have progressed and grown from that phase, now with the knowledge that when somebody wins, it does not necessarily mean someone must lose. Justin has somehow discovered a way to defy the zero-sum rule of economic game theory. The premise of game theory is that every winner must be counterbalanced with an equal and opposite loser. Justin has found a loophole in this theory, learning how to progress himself without stepping on others. As other folks may pull other people down to push him/herself up, he has cultivated a method to advance and succeed on his own without being at the expense of hindering another's development. As mentioned, Justin's only true competition is to be a better man than he was yesterday.

    I have looked up to Justin as a role model for many years—to lead; to joke; to reprimand; to guide—but never have I desired to emulate his specific acts. My goal has always been to borrow his admirable character traits and adopt them into my individual character and utilize them in my own specific and unique way of living. A true leader shows how to do something—not tells what exactly to do. In my eyes, and many others as we will soon explore, Justin embodies the meaning of a leader. He also embodies the true meaning of an older brother. There is a certain bond between two brothers unlike any other relationship on this planet. It is one of those situations where words do not serve the underlying concept of justice—brotherhood must be experienced to comprehend the meaning of the word wholly.

CAMERON JAMES WILLIAMS

Golden Ticket to the Backseat

For as long as I can remember—even from an extremely young age—Justin has always received the utmost respect from his peers and surrounding individuals. He has always embraced the knack of getting along with everybody. By no means was or is Justin an introvert, but reserved may be a more appropriate adjective. Also, not in the slightest was or is he argumentative, but when conflict did arise—if he spoke—99% (sorry Justin, you aren't getting the other percent) of the time he was correct, justified, and provided a valid point (some things just don't change). Whether at home, during a sporting event, or in a school setting, one thing remained constant: Justin treated others the same, no matter their age or identity, and they treated him with a reciprocated high level of respect. One of my faintest memories of this sustained reverence was in elementary school. I was in 1st grade while Justin was in 5th. The way our specific schooling system operated was grades K-5 were classified as elementary school, grades 6-8 middle school, and 9th grade through 12th grade was the high school tier. This meant that 5th graders were the cat's meow of their isolated kingdom. A handful of the students benevolently accepted the role of being idolized by the younger, less experienced students. While others utilized the opportunity to impose their superiority upon the more vulnerable pupils in lower grades. Whether on the playground, in the cafeteria, or on the bus—whatever the case—5th graders received the golden treatment and they knew it. As a 1st grader at the time, 5th graders were perceived as and compared to the likes of giants from an unknown world, while I was an ant waiting to be squashed by a stampede. Granted, there was few and far between occasions where a 1st grader was directly bullied by an older student, but regardless, there was a feeling of inferiority amongst my classmates and me. The standard rule of thumb is that the younger students defer to the older ones. On the bus, this meant that 5th graders occupied the back of the bus while 1st graders crammed into the seats up front behind the driver.

For me, things were different. As a 1st grader, I welcomed the opportunity and privilege of sitting in the back of the bus with the 5th graders. With Justin as my seat partner, I gained the authorization of his fellow classmates to sit in the back of the bus nearly every day to and from school. At the time, I was convinced the reason for my allowance was due to a unique skill of sorts I possessed. In 1st grade, I acquired the ability to expel gas on command. The 5th graders could not possibly receive enough of this entertainment. They were like a drug addict chasing the high from the first hit. Once they witnessed the magic initially, it became a daily occurrence on the way home from school. I don't mean to toot (pun intended) my own horn, but I must say I am even impressed of my prior (and unfortunately lost) talent to this day. But I came to realize years later the actual reason I was qualified to sit in the back of the bus in 1st grade, and it was not because I could flatulate upon request. In fact, any act or thing I said or did would have went over well. The real reason my young self was permitted to settle in the back of the bus was because of Justin. His fellow classmates and friends accepted and respected me because they respected him. A 1st grader sitting with 5th graders was unheard of, but if Justin silently gave the thumbs up, everybody else knew it was okay. And he never prompted anything through fear—it was simply the fact that his peers respected him as much or more than they respected anybody. I knew there was an underlying reason to this.

It is like the question: What came first, the chicken or the egg? In this case: What came first, the respect given to Justin or Justin demanding respect through his actions? And I think the appropriate response is that Justin gained a deep level of reverence solely for being himself. What you see is what you get with Justin. He was raised by our parents on superb moral standards, but since he is not very religious or flamboyantly spiritual, I am sure he rarely thinks of the Golden Rule taught in childhood, "Treat others how you want to be treated." But I am certain he embodies it each and every moment of every single day.

The pure acceptance I was blessed with in 1st grade carried on throughout all my years in school. A drastic (and perhaps far-fetched) parallel to the recognition received from holding the same last name as Justin is comparable to that of mafia ties in the past. According to the books I've read and movies watched relating to the mob, a last name can carry an immense amount of weight and paid great dividends in regards to the decision-making of others. Now, by no means was the abundance of Justin's sway proportional to the degree of John Gotti, but one could certainly draw a similarity. In any case, the validation I received from being Justin's brother was apparent to me. My personal golden ticket to the backseat is only a single instance where the Williams name provided immediate legitimacy.

The Williams Name

Through the entirety of my schooling years, when teachers read the Williams name on the roll call sheet aloud, there was an increased sense of enthusiasm. Like night follows day—if the teacher previously taught Justin in the classroom and recognized the last name—when nearing the letter *W* toward the end of the sheet, the tone of the instructor transformed from a monotone pitch to a liberating and inspired tune. "Here," I announced, putting my hand in the air when my name was called. Pausing, looking at me, and then back at the sheet again, the teacher would almost always make it a point to inquire or comment on Justin being my brother. "Are you as smart as your brother?" or "Your brother was one of my favorite students" were common questions or remarks I received at the beginning of each school year. A very similar kind of excitement and esteem diffused into the students in the school when mentioning Justin as well. He was dubbed the nicknames 'J-Willy' and 'Wills' in high school. Naturally, among other students and my peers, I assumed the nicknames 'C-Willy' and 'Little Wills.' Evidently, I had big shoes to fill. While not even consciously realizing it at the time—without an ounce of jealousy or pressure—I naturally experienced a rush of inspiration to be great when I heard the comments relating to my brother from teachers and students.

I pondered that if he had the ability to leave this type of a positive impression on people—while maintaining and demanding respect and honor—surely, I possessed the power inside me to manifest a similar influential mentality of behaving with greatness.

What you see is what you get with Justin. How he acts and lives in public remains constant behind closed doors. While always looking to find comic relief, he tows the line between work and play. When it is in fact time to bear down and get serious, his focus and execution are second to none. There is an economic theory called Preference Falsification formulated by social scientist Timur Kuran. The entirety of the theory is described in his book *Private Truths, Public Lies*. The premise of the theory is that preference falsification "is the act of misrepresenting one's wants under perceived social pressures. It happens frequently in everyday life, such as when we tell the host of a dinner party that we are enjoying the food when we actually find it bland."[1] Kuran's principle is also vastly apparent in government, corporations, and individuals. For example, some males wear a genuine and gentleman-like facade when courting a female, but in reality, they are actually misogynistic and only act a certain way to entice a woman to have sexual intercourse. In essence, the theory states that the public image and motivation of an individual or group may not mirror the private, actual intentions of said person or people.

However, this is not the case whatsoever with Justin—and it never has been. Unassailably few people, if any, talk badly about him when he is not in the room. In large part, this is why he was practically friends with everyone—at the very least positively acquainted—throughout his schooling years. As hinted to previously, Justin never displayed the personality of a true introvert but also could not be characterized as an extrovert either. In 8th grade—partially due to his friendly relations with others and, while the other portion was because of his distinctive brilliance in and out of the classroom—he was voted 'most likely to succeed' by his fellow classmates. I recall that he viewed the award at face value and nonchalantly panned it off like it wasn't a big deal. Winning the recognition sought after by many of his peers was somewhat ironic, because he never cared (and still doesn't) what anyone thought of him. Whether the president or a janitor was praising or criticizing him he took either as a grain of salt, and his levelheadedness allowed him to accept both ends of the spectrum objectively. In any situation, he gathered the positive aspects for his benefit and abandoned the negatives that didn't serve him. Justin's emotional disconnectedness through objectivity is a character trait of his I hold in high regard.

An example of this—also occurring in 8th grade—happened during the presidential race for class representatives. Initially, Justin chose to campaign for the position of class president, as he always set the standard high for himself. Due to his exceedingly infectious confidence, I remember having the feelings as if he was elected for the presidency before he even officially started running. I recall later that week he was hurled into a predicament—one of his close friends had made the choice to run for president as well. Justin relayed to my family and me that the kid was investing a great deal of stock into winning the class president position. After surveying his options, he arrived at a conclusion for his plan of action. Instead of running the risk of ruining a quality friendship while duking it out with his opponent for the presidency, Justin gallantly deferred to his comrade and decided to campaign for the vice president role. As tempting as I'm sure the ego must have been telling Justin to disregard the friendship and go for gold, his pragmatic and unpretentious nature led him to this compromise.

Justin's gifted in knowing when and why to pick a battle—and in the race for class presidency—the risk was not worth the reward. Referring back to Justin's unique ability to defy the game theory in economics, his choice to settle for vice presidency was a win-win scenario for both his friend and him. His friend, who desperately wanted to win the presidency position—and would have been heartbroken if he hadn't—ended up fulfilling his desires and winning the election for president. And Justin, on the other hand, avoided a conflict and also won the election in a landslide fashion for the vice presidency—still with the honors of being elected to the student council (The main reason he wanted to serve on the student council was for resume purposes in the future; not to enhance his sense of self-worth). There was no harm and no foul: Both Justin and his friend were happily chosen onto the student council, and they remained close friends. Whether or not his friend ever acknowledged or was even informed of Justin's reason for adjournment directly, I am sure his utmost appreciation was or would have been evident.

In that instance, I realized that I either originally misunderstood Justin's age-old saying, "If you're cheating, you're trying," or maybe he had matured and grew further to an even more so unashamedly honest and noble nature. Like I said, it's blatantly obvious that Justin would never actually cheat. Perhaps he actually genuinely did mean all those years, "I am going to do whatever it takes within moral and virtuous guidelines to achieve my goal." Or phrased another way, "I am going to give everything in my power towards the task at hand without slighting anyone." I am aware he was only thirteen or fourteen years old at the time of the student council occurrence, but his character has rung true and has only enhanced and progressed since time immemorial.

Just as Horatius righteously stood at the bridge for his family and country, Justin has always proudly represented and honored the Williams name passed down to him from our father, and his father, and so forth. Whether in the classroom or on the playing field, the level of respect and dignity reverberated towards Justin never wavered. "One who is transparent in words and action, commands confidence and respect. He takes decision with strength without being biased or prejudiced. One who lacks in transparency invites controversy with deep sense of distrust for the person"[2] is a quote from Dr. Anil Kumar Sinha that pretty much sums up Justin's temperament in the past and present and also touches on Timur Kuran's theory of Preference Falsification. Justin has always lived beyond his years and matured more fluently than his peers. In part due to his supportive upbringing from my parents, and another part from the innate power deep within him to be great, he has always excelled from the pack and led by example. Obvious in trivial situations—such as running for student council in middle school—and extending to scenarios as monumental as making the conscious choice to embark on the 2650 mile journey of the Pacific Crest Trail—he has proven and continues to prove one thing true: Respect is earned; not given.

CAMERON JAMES WILLIAMS

CHAPTER 3: A MAN AS A BOY

"The only limits in our life are those we impose on ourselves"[1] is a concise yet powerful line from motivational speaker and self-help expert Bob Proctor. As with any other quote, the words are only a signpost to the underlying truth and meaning that are hidden under them. But these twelve words in their specific order encompass a world of truth and meaning within them. Justin graciously understands this meaning. In the current section, we will explore how Justin has pushed—and still pushes—the limits in his everyday life. Whether within himself as a whole, with his mind and intellect, or physical body, as well within his own discipline and self-respect, Justin lives without boundaries and presses the envelope to find his breaking point—and then goes beyond it. To his credit, he searches diligently to seek and destroy these self-imposed limits Bob Proctor speaks of, be it testing himself in the most trivial of matters or spanning to flirt with danger as a result of uncontrollable variables—such as Mother Nature and the Pacific Crest Trail. As confident as he is in his abilities and self, he respects Mother Nature to the highest degree and is aware that her forces will prevail ten out of ten times. The dichotomy and balance between unwavering pride and utmost humility is truly beautiful to observe, and in my case, experience with Justin. Whatever the situation, if Justin immerses himself into it, one thing is guaranteed; he will put his best foot forward and give all his effort. As we will learn in the following paragraphs and sections, pushing limits is the pure essence of what it means to be alive.

Pushing limits is a conscious choice. Pushing limits is the seed planted that sows progression. There is no room to worry, doubt, or sulk when pushing limits. It is not for the faint-hearted or the glass half-empty type of people. Pushing limits requires the unique perspective and propensity to see a glass as overflowing with abundance when in fact it is simply half full. It is surrendering the image and boundary of self to be a part of something much more powerful and grander in scale. Pushing limits involves sacrificing blood, sweat, and tears all for an unknown outcome. Steve Jobs of Apple, Horatius at the bridge, and the Founding Fathers understood the meaning of this sacrifice. So did Jesus Christ when he stood inexorably in front of Pilate; Nelson Mandela when dismantling the legacy of the apartheid; Martin Luther King Jr when fighting for equality; as well as Nicholas Copernicus when he boldly and shamelessly proposed that the sun was

THE 2650 MILE AISLE

the center of the Universe in 1543; or Thomas Edison with his invention of the lightbulb when he continued trying after his 999th failed attempt; and Christopher Columbus when sailing the ocean blue, bravely discovering (perhaps re-discovering is the more proper term, but that's a different story for a different day) the New World in 1492. The list throughout history continues on but one theme is prevalent and apparent across all of these individuals' actions: The fearless faith to contribute to something greater than the self outweighed the uncertainty of outcome and any sort of doubt or negativity. With that being said, I'm sure pushing the limits—even for these noble individuals—was a continuous struggle and no easy task. But their undying courageous spirits and immortality of contributions made every ounce of energy and sacrifice worth it—even if they could not see the plentiful results and infinite sowing that ensued from the seeds planted. In all of these cases, as well as with Justin, the respect earned did not come first. Initially, the margins were stress-tested and perhaps plowed through, and then the objective soul's deserved and earned respect resulted from the bold actions. Pushing limits is not a flip that can be turned on and off inside of an individual; it is deeply embedded into one's character.

The title of this chapter, "A Man as a Boy," is a symbol of the maturity, courage, confidence, and selflessness necessary to look beyond the current perceived drudgery and have faith in the greatness, progression, and potential of the present moment. The title refers back to the point of trusting one's self fully right now while also simultaneously having faith in something greater beyond the crest that can't be seen. To push limits is to grow, and to grow is to live. Another way to word pushing limits is progression, and progression is essentially the constant transformation of fear into courage leading to continuous growth. We will explore how Justin, even as a young boy, has pushed limits and fast-tracked his expansion into a literal and metaphorical man. And the narrative does not stop here, because pushing the limits is an infinite and perennial quest. Every moment is an ongoing test to remove the self-imposed boundaries within and without. Adding to that, each moment should not be viewed as a means to something else. Rather each moment contains utmost fulfillment in itself, independent from any other moment. Through intelligence, with wit, by utilizing brute strength, as well as patience and discipline, Justin has established access of the portal to this limitless and formless place. While examining past occurrences as well as motives, we will gain an enhanced understanding and insight into how and why this access is possible—to Justin as well as all of us.

Camping: A Call to the Wild

Camping has always been an annual tradition in the Williams family. Whether pitching a tent to sleep in, or later on—in our more comfortable nights—sleeping in a pop-up camper that we hauled using a car, we always enjoyed a peaceful weekend in the woods. There is something indescribably special about Mother Nature in how she demands an individual's peace, presence, and sense of wonder when in her domain. She indiscriminately continuously creates and changes the world, not caring about gender, race, age, credence, or any other falsely perceived human variance.

Yes, I'm sure there were petty arguments at some point amongst my siblings and myself those weekends, but in the wilderness, they were always a little less harsh and certainly more short-lived. It's as if Mother Nature whispered, "Calm down my children. There is no need to fight. Just be still." as a gust of wind blew past and suddenly we were back to cracking jokes and telling stories by the campfire. Perhaps the reason for this peace and wonder is due to the fact of the vastness of a forest and nature herself. It is like looking up into the stars on a perfectly clear night, when the realization sinks in of how minuscule we are as humans compared to the grandness of the Universe. All the trivial worries and self-imposed perceived issues of life fade away as you become a part of something bigger. A stillness remains—as the mind stops its race—and a feeling of gratitude and presence wash over the soul as the body feels weightless. Looking out into a forest in the morning when camping—just as the sun is rising and the world is awakening, although never actually sleeping—as birds chirp near and far with the dewy grass kissing your toes, is akin to the sense of stillness and peace of gazing into the galaxy. Perhaps camping is where Justin's faculty of wonder and exploration was initially realized. Perhaps Mother Nature sat him down one morning when he was fishing and talked to him. Perhaps she spoke to him in her mysterious, indirect way; by the chirping of the birds above his head; the bustling of the leaves around his feet; or by the sun glowing just right in a clear blue sky, positioned up above his whole world. Perhaps that is the moment when he surrendered the image of himself to merge with something immeasurable that contains no boundaries—and felt at home.

Whatever be the case, Justin has always been his freest and in his most precious and simplest form in the woods. From the time we pulled into the spot to the moment we packed up all the food and supplies, he was chomping at the bit to enjoy Mother Nature to her fullest capacity. Justin in the woods was, and still is, like a kid in a candy store. Whether it was starting fires, fishing, carving sticks, constructing snares—or even helping our dad set the campsite up, Justin's presence met the task fully with precision as the result. We have camped for as long as I can remember, and for as long as I can remember Justin has acted the same way in the wilderness. Even today when we go camping—nothing has changed—he continues to possess the deepest sort of reverence towards nature while also pushing her limits to the furthest degree. Unlike in the makeshift soccer game created the one July 4th weekend (the one when I was eventually body-slammed by Justin), Mother Nature is one place where Justin understands her unquestionable rules and would never think about tweaking them. He knows that she will win that battle ten out of ten times. The balance between Justin's respect and finesse in relation to Mother Nature is a gorgeous thing to witness and be a part of.

    For hours at a time—after scaling the forest in its entirety in search for a perfect stick—he would carve a stick while sitting by the campfire. Using his ten-dollar pocket knife from the camp store, each shaving of bark he stroked off was like his life depended on it. "Justin, take a break and eat some lunch," my parents frequently suggested, as he continued without skipping a beat, completely immersed in his masterpiece. There was a conscious method chosen from start to finish for every aspect of carving the stick, from finding a stick with enough durability and length while also being lightweight to the finishing touches of etching indentations in the top of the stick for a handle. The precision involved, and energy put forth into his craft, was as if the stick was being carved in hopes of winning an Olympic medal. But this was not a competition with other carvers, and nor did Justin view his carving in this light. He enjoyed the quest of finding the stick just as much as he had of sculpting a razor-sharp point on the finalized stick.

In Justin's mind, the finalized stick was already manifested before he even ventured down to the camp store to purchase the knife. It was simply a matter of bringing it into existence, in which he would do scrupulously or wouldn't even do it at all. I can imagine watching him carve that stick (that still remains in the garage) was equivalent to how it would be watching Van Gogh paint *Starry Night*—the individuals focusing on every detail while keeping the entire piece of art in mind; the individuals pushing their abilities to their full capacities and beyond in determination to achieve perfection; and the selflessness encapsulated in the work—for surely that stick was not created for Justin nor that painting for Van Gogh's sake. This type of precision in action became so normal and second nature to Justin that I am not certain if he even remembers that carved stick or not. But from the outside looking in, my family members and I were mesmerized by the artisanship invoked into such an inconsequential act. Whatever the act, be it big or small in importance, Justin expressed this exact attitude and effort toward anything he approached in life—wringing out the full value at hand.

    Fishing and starting campfires were no exception to this for Justin in the woods. Waking up at six in the morning, he would bolt down to the lake to cast a line when the fish were hungry for breakfast and before the influx of boats towing water skiers commenced for the day, that left the waters choppy and undesirable to fish on. Preparing his fishing-rod the day before, he was ready to rock and roll when he woke up the following morning. I swear sometimes he was so eager to start fishing he made it down to his chair by the water before he even emptied his bladder. Fishing to Justin was and still is an art form. While aware of the uncontrollable factors in fishing—the potential of there not being fish in a specific area, or they just might not be hungry that day—he considers every other controllable variable. Employing his intellect and a resourceful utilization of the internet, he plans and studies accordingly for fishing before going camping. Before initially casting a fishing line for a weekend, a game plan is in mind. Whether it's playing the odds of knowing that one fish might prefer live bait in the morning while another favors a lure in the evening; or that certain fish live toward the surface of the water while others occupy the depths of the more frigid lake floor, he strategizes accordingly to maximize the amount of fish reeled to the shore. Although I recall some days when fishing, knowing he put his best foot forward, he would come back to camp empty-handed with a smile on his face—just as content as the previous day when he carried a stringer full of bass and trout behind his back. He carried on with his nature-packed day, not leaving a second in his mind to dwell on the lack of fish caught earlier that morning. After organizing his fishing rod and supplies for the next endeavor to the water, Justin would usually start a fire as the remaining family members were waking from their slumber.

    Justin orchestrated his campfires with the same rigor as any other task he undertook. First, he would scavenge the forest floor for kindling. His scavenging would have made proud the character Goldilocks from the famous fairytale *Goldilocks and the Three Bears*—that twig was too small, and that twig was too big—the twigs Justin returned to camp with were just right (Except unlike Goldilocks, Justin was granted permission from Mother Nature to do so). Stepping out of the pop-up, rubbing the morning gook out of my eyes, I often remember blinking awake and seeing Justin carefully and gently caressing the pile of sticks—like a mother carrying her first newborn—on his way back to the fire pit. After laying the kindling down in the middle of the pit, he judiciously gathered the larger pieces of firewood and placed them next to the fire pit, ready to stack on top of the kindling. If the logs were too large, he chopped them with an ax to what he thought was the most efficient, appropriate size. Once his metaphoric ducks were in a line, he would light the kindling and blow ever so gently into his deliberately chosen twigs until they were engulfed in flames. Simultaneously, he stacked the medium-sized pieces of wood onto the enflamed kindling in a criss-cross fashion—leaving enough space so the fire would not smother—and positioned them close enough to each other so they would still catch fire. Once again Goldilocks would be proud. While continuing to provide oxygen by elegantly huffing and puffing without blowing the house of fire down (the Big Bad Wolf won't approve here but at least Goldilocks does), the flames multiplied, and the fire organically grew in size.

    Alas, Justin remaining crouched and one with the fire—staying as close as he could to the heat without burning—still tried to find a way to improve the flames. He would then situate the largest logs in a teepee-like fashion around the already lit foundation of kindling and medium-sized logs. Moments later, the fire was complete as the controlled inferno was blazing towards the sky. As the wood crackled deep within, sending embers shooting to the heavens, Justin would give one final powerful and deep, oceanic sounding breath into the fire—engulfing every single piece of lumber in a burning sea of red, orange, and blue hues. Standing from his crouch, he would nonchalantly walk away from the flames to the cooler to grab a drink of ice-cold water and continue on with his day.

The rest of the family normally stationed themselves by the fire at this point, enjoying the fruits of Justin's labor. Justin would eventually sit down, and my sister or dad resumed the conversation or spooky story from the night before. Every so often when the fire was dwindling, one of us would feed the fire a few more logs—completely appreciating the fire—but more than likely not thinking of the scavenging for kindling in the woods, or the ax-splitting an hour prior. There is something sacred about congregating in the presence of fire; feeling both the soothing warmth and relentlessness of the flames at the same time. By the time breakfast was eaten, Justin was usually off exploring into the forest.

The one year, I remember Justin hatched the idea of architecting a snare deep in the woods. That same year, previous to the camping trip, Justin was a gifted a survival book for Christmas. In it taught how to gut an animal, how to start a fire, equipment necessary to survive in the wilderness—and also how to make a snare. He diligently read the book front to back, but that was only the first step. In typical Justin fashion, reading about how to construct a snare was not sufficient to him—he had to actually make one himself. And that is exactly what he set out to do.

I recall this project he undertook was accomplished in a single day. He gathered some rope and a few other items and began his mission early in the morning (I'm not sure if he even went fishing that day). Justin searched far and wide for the most favorable snare-making tree. It needed to be flexible enough to bend to the ground while being sturdy enough not to snap if a small animal, such as a raccoon, was captured. In the distance, after traversing back and forth through the dense woods for an hour or two, just as I was losing sight of Justin, I faintly saw him finally settle at a tree about a quarter or half-mile away. It must have been the one he was foraging for. Upon reaching that special tree, Justin immediately got to work. I saw the outline of a boy gazing up at a tree he had his hands on, but it looked more like an engineer gathering around the initial construction of the Empire State Building. My family and I remained at the campsite—playing cards, eating food, making smores, and cracking more jokes—while Justin answered his call to the wild.

After five or six hours, he returned with an uncontrollable smirk on his face. "Hey, Justin is back," my dad said. And before words emptied out of Justin's mouth, my family, and I anticipated what he was about to say and already stood up out of our chairs and started walking towards the woods. "I'm going to grab some peanut butter to use to bait animals to the snare." As one big happy family with Justin leading the way to his creation, we ventured off the beaten path through the forest to the newly engineered snare.

We arrived at the snare, and in awe we stood in silence for a minute—of which felt like an eternity. It was the most beautiful thing to see standing in the middle of the woods. I looked to the left, to the right, ahead, and behind at the neighboring trees in the forest that were all in their original form. Then looking back at Justin's masterpiece, I felt the alchemy, energy, resilience, and strength of the snare that was not there the day before. The tree was just the right diameter, being flexible yet strong. To this day, I'm not sure if Justin found the tree or if the tree found Justin. And of course, the rope was snipped to the exact length needed. Then it was tied to the top portion of the tree, with a knot forming a loop at the end of it that hovered ever so slightly below the leaves. It felt as if the snare should have been in a museum with a 'Please Do Not Touch' sign planted in front of it. The snare embodied pure creation. Justin initially approached a tree that previously had not been very useful to him and transformed it into a completely different, useful object. He accepted the creation of the tree from Mother Nature and metamorphosed it into something that took a separate form and nature. The snare, whose image is still clear as day in my head, was an act of pure alchemy and creation.

As my family and I huddled around the snare, Justin, with a spoon and jar of peanut butter in hand, started to envelop the rope in hopes of attracting a hungry animal native to the specific area. After his delicate lathering of peanut butter, we all walked back to the campsite together. Food and card games awaited us, so that's what we indulged in. It was our last night of camping, so we would find out if the snare captured anything the next day. Although I had not partaken in the creation, I think I carried more angst regarding the snare catching an animal than Justin did, as he had not mentioned his work of art the entire evening. The next day, before packing up to leave, Justin checked the snare and there had not been a sign of a hungry animal. With the utmost respect toward Mother Nature and superior sportsmanship he constantly possessed, Justin carefully disassembled the snare and headed back to camp. But whether he captured an animal wasn't of any importance to him. Justin exercised everything in his realm of power and was content with the outcome regardless. No matter what, Justin always left camp with a grin and returned the same way.

Pushing the Limits of Intellect

Pushing the limits is a broad, umbrella statement that encompasses a more general outlook and meaning. Within the statement contains many different particular aspects underneath that in their own way define or contribute to the phrase—albeit in a more concise, specific sense. One of these precise forms encapsulated in the phrase in its entirety is pushing the limits of intellect, which is a particular portion within the general phrase. A similar comparison is the mathematic rule that all squares are considered rectangles but not all rectangles are technically squares. In our case, all pushing the limits of intellect fits under the phrase pushing the limits, but pushing the limits as a generalization does not invariably mean pushing the limits of intellect, the particularized utterance. Justin's pushing the limits of intellect will be the focus of this current section.

Justin has always pushed the boundaries of his brain and mental capacity. As a student of life, he's never stopped learning—but not in a so-called bookworm sense. Frankly, the boy and now man certainly did not expand his knowledge through reading books—unless forced to via academics (or chosen via survival books)—but rather learned and pushed his intellect through experience. Reading a book and attaining information through that book was only one aspect of learning in his eyes. Without the second part of action and actually putting the knowledge into practice, the information was essentially irrelevant to him. His outlook here refers back to the Lamborghini reference surfaced in Chapter 1. A person can read about how to drive a Lamborghini until he/she is blue in the face, but an individual who has actually driven the car possesses a far greater understanding of how to operate the vehicle, and the intricate details and variables that cannot be condensed into a text format.

Acquiring knowledge is great, but applying that knowledge is what allows the information to be useful. Justin's understanding of topics and skills penetrates deep to the source of any said situation. He not only understands each aspect of a topic on its own—but rather comprehends how each aspect works together to understand the topic in its entirety. A car mechanic may be an expert on both a radiator and transmission separately, but unless he/she understands how the components of a car work together to contribute to the operation of the whole car, the knowledge of the radiator and transmission matter not. Or if a doctor is not aware of the interconnectedness of the human body and, for instance, prescribes a heart medication that benefits the heart while negatively affecting the lungs, the medicine may have a net negative outcome for the patient.

Maintaining a deeper understanding of both specific components and also how they contribute to the whole of the object—in any category of life—is critical. Albert Einstein once said, "If you can't explain it to a six-year-old, you don't understand it yourself."[1] There is a great deal of truth in his proclamation and that statement pretty much sums up the point trying to be made here. Keeping this short phrase from Einstein in mind when pushing the limits of the intellect is imperative to progressing mentally. Justin, as a student of life, has always delved into the root of a topic—whether in school, interpreting historic information, as well as regarding wit and humor, among other things—to grasp a concept totally. In a very matter-of-fact way, he has a knack to be able to simplify the most complex of topics. Let's take a look at a few examples and instances where this ability is illustrated and may have arisen from.

    I, among many others, have the tendency that when I purchase an item from the store that needs assembled—whether a piece of furniture or a technological device—I dive right into configuring the parts of said object. Upon ripping the box open, I toss the instruction manual aside, and start connecting components that look like they should be connected together. I use a trial-and-error type approach—only referring to the instruction manual if absolutely necessary. To my demise—saving the extra five to ten minutes to not read and comprehend the instructions before diving into configuration—I usually spend more time in the end backtracking and correcting the mistakes I just made. This type of character trait is comparable to the hare in the moral fable *The Tortoise and the Hare*.

Justin is comparable to the likes of the tortoise in the fable. He keeps the end goal in mind and methodically focuses on one step at a time to reach a certain destination. With respect to Justin when he purchases a piece of furniture, upon opening the box, he will digest the instruction manual entirely before jumping into assembling the chair or sofa. First and foremost, Justin will understand the purpose of each element on its own, and then he will understand how each component works together to benefit the function of the object in its totality. But Justin does not view the initial process as a chore. He finds enjoyment in acquiring knowledge on how each piece of the puzzle is useful to the grander scale—in this case, a piece of furniture. And when all is said and done, he usually properly assembles a couch faster than somebody like me who figures out the process on the fly. Both methods reach the same destination, but the former one is substantially more efficient, and ultimately more effective. Justin's outlook on life, as well as furniture assembling, loosely but accurately relates to the quote, "Give a man a fish, you feed him for a day. Teach a man how to fish and you feed him for the rest of his life."[2] Knowledge is definitely power—but application of knowledge is even more powerful better yet.

Justin's habits and character relative to pushing the limits of his intellect were always evident at museums as well. Until recently—when I slowly but surely adopted a different approach and perspective—I was always the individual to not find much interest at museums. I would breeze through each exhibit, briefly surveying each statue or painting, and then moving on to the next one swiftly. By doing this I gained a superficial and vague understanding of the objects being looked at. Consequently, my depth of comprehension was extremely shallow because the significant substance that existed below the surface was where the importance lived. At a fleeting glance, this importance was missed as the next exhibit already flooded my mind. No doubt were museums cool and interesting, but the value absorbed was only a sliver of the whole pie. Instead of enjoying each exhibit on its own and lending it my entire presence, my mind was already jumping to the next form of stimulation.

Justin has always taken the opposite approach when observing the art or history at museums. Each description or background text of a painting or sculpture was read and apprehended thoroughly first. And then the object being viewed was perceived in a more penetrative manner, absorbing the full value of said object. By taking the time to first soak in each piece of literature—and then looking at the statue afterwards, connecting the dots of what was read to what was seen—he was more aligned with the total substance of the exhibit. He patiently enjoyed each exhibit—not looking ahead nor looking back—immersed in presence with each painting or statue. In a revolutionary war type portion of a museum, it was as if he imagined himself as Samuel Adams dumping tea into the Boston Harbor. It appeared as if he could feel the breeze blowing off of the harbor; and smell the tea being dumped in the middle of the night; and feel the pen that signed the Declaration of Independence; and taste the ale processed in one of the thirteen colonies. Standing upright gazing at the colonial figure after reading the history, time did not exist as he attempted to mentally emulate the experience from many years ago of the American symbol perching in front of him.

Once again—just like the approach to assembling furniture from him and me—the same act is taking place but in completely separate manners, with evidently varying experiences. The details of these, on the surface seemingly trivial manners, are where a world of differing outcomes for an individual exists. I, in the Samuel Adams instance, experienced a neat looking sculpture, whereas Justin's experience was vastly divergent and provided a substantially more beneficial and long-lasting result. I was metaphorically reading how to drive a Lamborghini when Justin was taking the car for a ride around the track.

CAMERON JAMES WILLIAMS

His passion for thrusting the limits of his mind carried over into the television he consumed throughout his childhood and teen years as well. Justin was never one to become engrossed into mindless reality TV series, as he quickly realized that doing so would rapidly lead to the destruction of brain cells. Rather, he preferred intellectually stimulating programs, such as documentaries. His two favorite television networks were indisputably the History Channel and Discovery Channel, frequently tuning into shows such as *Modern Marvels* or Les Stroud's *Survivorman*. But perhaps a sleeper pick for Justin's most-watched television show was *How It's Made* on the Science Channel, since he was always interested in breaking down the design of anything into its simplest form. The Discovery Channel and History Channel (as well as the Science Channel) challenged Justin to think for himself about the newer, more enhanced information being presented. Some of the concepts depicted in a historical documentary—such as about Nazi, Germany—were foreign initially, before he consciously absorbed the information being shown until he understood it. Even if the topic of discussion was more advanced beyond his complete interpretation, he continued to watch and learn as much as possible at the time. A parallel of a younger boy watching a series of history programs beyond his full comprehension can be compared to the likes of an individual repetitively watching the *Harry Potter* movies instead of reading the books. The intricate details may not be understood or recognized at first, but the theme, general plotline, and common elements are eventually capable of being properly grasped and connected more wholly. Similarly, after watching a multitude of advanced documentaries on the same topic, Justin was subsequently competent enough to put two and two together. He was then qualified to take his freshly acquired knowledge a step further and correlate and relate the history of the past to the present times. It was at the margin of testing his intellectual boundaries where Justin learned to progress beyond them. By enacting this sequence routinely Justin not only enhanced the ability of his mind but also his abilities as a human being in general. Even at a young age, Justin seemed to understand the profound philosopher, Socrates, who once said, "I only know that I know nothing."[3] But that's how he learned to learn.

    Justin's third favorite network to tune into was no doubt Comedy Central, gravitating towards programs such as *South Park* or *Workaholics*. Justin has always appreciated comedy and humor. Irony, wit, and intellect truly go hand and hand. To understand the source of where wit or a joke is derived, one must be intellectually savvy. And all things considered, irony is simply doing or saying the opposite of what is expected. It is unquestionably a skill. Justin was always responsive to a well-thought-out joke or comedy skit. He realized and appreciated the essence of how the joke or skit was formulated. His underlying conception and knowledge of wit is a large part of how his humor is so effective in day-to-day life as well. The timing, substance, and depth of Justin's jokes are second to none. Part of this ability is from watching comedy shows, but most of it is the richer understanding of where this wit stems from.

Justin never watched a show just to watch it. When he watched television, it was for one of two reasons: to learn or to laugh. The balanced approach of training the left and right sides of his brain—the analytical and creative portions, respectively—is how he reaped the rewards of continuous growth for his brain and intellect. By persistently pushing the limits of his intellect, Justin was able to expand not only his mind, but his aptitude to push the limits of life in general.

Pushing the Limits of Body

As we've learned already, pushing the limits of life is manifested in a slew of varying specific forms. One of the forms, as seen above, is pushing the limits of intellect. Another particular form under the umbrella of the more generalized principle of pushing the limits of life—which will be the focus of the current section—is pushing the limits of the body. Just as pushing the limits of intellect is not an all-encompassing example of pushing the limits of life, pushing the limits of the body is a singular stroke of the brush contributing to the painting of greater magnitude. With that being said, Justin's pressing of boundaries regarding his physical body is, in fact, a microcosm and insight into the grander macrocosm of the general principle at hand. Stated another way, a drop of water from the sea nearly replicates any other specific droplet therein, but when magnified we don't refer to that one drop as the whole ocean. Only when all the drops are unified does it prompt us to note the totality of the body of water. Yet, the single drop from the ocean contains the same exact substance and elements as the undivided sea. In Justin's case, the character illustrated when pushing the limits of his body transcends the specific act and correlates to his pushing of the universal limits of life.

CAMERON JAMES WILLIAMS

One of the examples that stands out in my memory of him testing his physical boundaries was in the athletic weight room when in high school. Nearly ten years ago at this point, I still remember the occurrence clear as day. Justin has always been drawn to the activity of lifting weights. But it was never to impress anyone via bulging toned biceps and a shredded chest—propping up the egotistical self. Nor was it to continuously boast to others about how much he worked out, which also protects the fragile image of self through the approval of peers. Rather, he lifted weights for the objective purpose of performing better on the field or at the ice rink—becoming stronger, more agile, and increasing endurance. Considering Justin's enhanced mental capacity, he deduced his rational thoughts to the realization that if he was able to squat or bench more weight, then that would smoothly translate to on the field when pushing a defensive lineman backwards off the line of scrimmage. When he was in the gym, it was for the sole function of improving his physical abilities on the field. At the same, somewhat paradoxically, he enjoyed the actual process of progressing physically as much as he was enthused of improving the results on the playing field, which was the chief aim at the time.

The magnificent feat I recall is when he leg-pressed 1000 pounds. The one day he came home and casually mentioned to the family how he surpassed his personal record on the leg press exercise. We congratulated him and asked what the maximum amount of weight the other members on the team propelled into the air with their legs. He was clueless to the numerical weights his teammates lifted but did mention in a matter-of-fact manner that his thousand pounds set the team record. He was less concerned with what his fellow peers hoisted but more thrilled on the detail that he trumped his own record from the previous year. With that so, Justin was content with the achievement for the time being, nevertheless recognizing he could still push his body further. The next day he already calibrated his sights on exceeding the 1250-pound milestone. Typical to Justin's mindset, he understood progression was ultimately infinite—not only in relation to testing perceived restraints of the physical body—but also in the pushing of life's boundaries in general.

Pushing the Limits of Willpower

Our final distinct examination of Justin's power to exceed the self-imposed limits and barriers of life is specifically relative to that of testing the extent of one's willpower. Another way of saying willpower is by substituting self-control. Yet another word synonymous is self-discipline. In any case, embodying whichever of the above three words—to a high order or not—is the difference between being conscious or unconscious, respectively. Demonstrating complete willpower entails alertness of the present moment to the most elevated degree. Whether a given situation is the most trivial of choices or a decision of significant importance, a highly objective, conscious approach yields the most beneficial results. Sometimes our emotions or thoughts tell us otherwise and steer us to a rash conclusion, but our unbiased intuition never fails us. Being closely in touch with our intuition and hearts—the truth—always leads us down the correct path when there is a fork in the road. Every action or inaction in life is a binary choice, and impartial willpower must remain evident as a determining factor. Justin undoubtedly grasped the prominence of willpower in life's incessant choices. There is no grey area here. One either chooses to do or he/she chooses not to do. Encircled in the choosing, self-control must shine bright, like the sun at the beach on a

THE 2650 MILE AISLE

warm summer day. So often as humans we allow our egos to convince and lie to our true, conscious selves of what the right thing to do is. When this happens, our lack of willpower is exposed, and an unconscious determination is the consequence. On the contrary, when our willpower is exercised to its full potential, a fruitful outcome is the result.

    Deep within, every single human being possesses the capacity to know the difference between right and wrong in any given situation. Whether we actualize this potential through willpower over the ego (i.e. consciousness vs unconsciousness; positive vs negative; God vs Devil; Heaven vs Hell; light vs dark) is a different story. Sometimes our heart tells us one thing and our body proceeds the exact opposite direction. That exemplifies a weakness of self-discipline. Justin lives on the reverse side of this coin. He will defer a sense of short-term, temporary satisfaction patiently knowing there is a long-term, eternal gratification beyond that initial point. The strength involved in resisting the mind and body's animal-like desires is a beautiful affair to witness.

    I had the privilege to experience Justin employing this strength of willpower after the prom dance when he was a senior in high school. Justin and his date for the evening attended a party at a cabin in the woods after the big dance. The cabin, from what I gathered, was filled to the brim with a good time. Everyone was letting loose and living for the night. As hyped up as prom is for students in high school, they were sure to make it an unforgettable night. Now, I am not saying there was underage alcohol consumption taking place at this party, but let's just say not everyone remembered this night when it was all said and done (cough, cough, wink, wink).

Finding all of this out from one of my brother's friends after the fact, I was told by her that Justin's date was one of the individuals who fell victim to overindulgence in the adult beverages. According to my brother's friend, she said that his date actually drank so much that she blacked out. Also, his friend mentioned how proud she was of Justin. She painted a picture for me of how Justin's date was begging for sexual intercourse amid her drunken stupor. She explained how Justin—even after three or four obvious attempts of his date enticing him—respectfully declined her sexual offerings because she was not in the proper state. I'm sure Justin, seventeen at the time, was inclined by his animal desires to proceed with the short-term satisfaction of sex. But his powerful self-discipline demanded otherwise, knowing deep down that taking advantage of somebody under the influence of alcohol would not have been the right thing to do. Justin, on that particular evening after prom—as he frequently shows in other instances—exemplified what pushing the limits of willpower truly means.

By being tested to make a decision, he consciously chose to ascend to higher, nobler ground above his ego. The selfless resolution was one of following the soul's intuition for the greater good. In his case, his mind and body were telling him one thing, but he declared "Nay" to the temptation and rose beyond it. Possessing the strength to resist temptations and primitive desires is the essence of pure willpower.

As with any assaying of limits in life, testing of one's willpower proves to be no different in its underlying nature. Whether pushing the limits of intellect, body, or self-discipline—one thing is true throughout—every limit exceeded, or test passed expands the horizon and ascends the individual to level-up from the state occupied prior. This leveling-up continues the infinite progression and evolution of a conscious being. Every checkpoint reached through the transcended form broadens elevated spheres of perception—effectually ushering in new limits to be exceeded and tests to be passed. But every specific level passed contributes to the well-being and ascension of the life form in general. At these boundaries is where everlasting growth and learning exist. Nevertheless, by no means is pushing the limits of life a so-called easy task. That said, it is one that is worthwhile and produces lifelong fulfillment—and what it means to truly be alive.

Pushing the limits of life is not for the faint-hearted or the weak-minded. Nor is it for fearful or diffident souls. Fear is, in fact, the second most powerful force in the Universe. The only thing more powerful than fear is courage. Courage is the bridge that, when crossed, leads to the bearing of life's eternal fruits that graciously await on the other side. But, almost seeming paradoxical, courage should not be used as a means to some end in the future but rather enjoyed for its own sake. All in all, living with courage and pushing the limits of life go hand-in-hand—both of which lead to a life overflowing with abundance.

CHAPTER 4: THE ONLY WAY IS THROUGH

As the title of this chapter suggests, the focal point and theme of the following narratives and examples illustrated by Justin revolve around two significant ideas. The general concepts to be depicted throughout this chapter are: how adversity is inevitable through life's endeavors, with persistence being a critical component of surpassing these obstacles; and also how confidence in one's self leads to a positive mindset and perspective in any given situation, ultimately warranting a belief, insight, and peace of mind to the individual towards the things that can and cannot be controlled in life. Both of these will be intertwined during this chapter—because in reality the two notions can't be separated to be understood fully. To victoriously battle adversity in its most practical sense, one must possess the utmost degree of self-confidence paired with a positive mindset. And vice versa, the extent of one's self-confidence and optimistic outlook is unable to be realized to its full capacity unless there is some sort of adversity at hand—which calls for an enhanced level of persistence to prevail.

Justin realized the above points at a very young age and constructed a sound foundation utilizing them—and today continues to lay the bricks and increase the solidarity regarding his metaphorical structure of self-confidence and ability to transcend adversity. When faced with an analogous brick wall in life—whether he has to go through it, around it, over it, or under it—Justin is positive he will successfully navigate to the other side. The Royal Air Force's Latin phrase. "Per aspera ad astra" is translated in English to, "Through adversity to the stars"[1] and touches on this vantage point elegantly, yet precisely. On the other side of adversity is an everlasting plentifulness encompassing prosperity and well-being. It takes an unwavering faith in one's self, coupled with a positive attitude, to battle adversity most effectively and maximize the reaping of benefits from the labor sowed beforehand. One may draw a parallel from this Latin phrase to the likes of removing a splinter from a finger. A splinter is required to be pulled out before the healing and reward of being pain-free can take place. If the splinter is not removed, it will continue to cause pain and drudgery to the individual in an endless loop of suffering and will never heal properly. It takes a small amount of pain to invoke a world of healing and peace. Adversity, or the splinter in the example, must be faced head-on and

THE 2650 MILE AISLE

trumped to usher in the abundance of life in its entirety—and in the splinter's case the healing process.

Justin has expressed his expertise in the field of self-confidence and persistence in various ways throughout his life. Whether through health conditions or by extreme tests to his faith in himself, he always handled the situation at hand accordingly. And I think 'handling the situation at hand' is one of his tricks and skills he's acquired to overcome the most undesirable of conditions. It really relates back to the concept of living in the present moment. Essentially the past and the future are illusions because the past was once the present moment and now is gone, and the future will be a present moment and will never arrive sooner than right now. Therefore, if one eternally lives utterly in the present moment or 'handles the situation at hand,' then the thought of past and future are irrelevant. To add to this concept further, if somebody—Justin in our case—is self-confident enough in him/herself, then stress, anxiety, regret, or any result of negativity will not exist either. Anxiety and worry derive from thoughts of uncontrollable scenarios in the future, and regret and anger are the results of living in and replaying the illusion of the past—which is set in stone. Now that is not to say Justin does not learn from his past or prepare for the future accordingly—but he does so in an extremely objective manner and is alert enough to realize the only thing he can control; his actions in the present moment.

In a phone call I recently had with Justin a few days before Miranda and his departure for the Pacific Crest Trail (which will be described in-depth in Chapter 7), he bluntly stated that life is full of actions and reactions. He elaborated on the fact that a majority of life is reacting to the present moment. He went on to say that our reactions to the events that happen in life are the only things we can truly control. How insightful and characteristic of Justin it was to explain the resolution to the hindrances of so many people's lives—stress and anxiety—in such an acutely concise and simplistic manner. There is a vast variety of situations and outcomes in life that cannot be controlled. Justin would agree that thinking endlessly about the uncontrollable—when trapped in the mind—is useless and a waste of energy. Doing this is like mimicking a hamster running on a wheel that continuously revolves, effectually with no progress being made as the result. Rather, when 100% of an individual's energy is focused on the controllable aspects of the present moment—anxiety, stress, regret, and anger dissipate into the ether.

On top of that, life becomes much simpler as a burdensome weight is lifted off the shoulders. The freedom and confidence of an individual is drastically increased because energy is no longer being pulled and divided into a million different directions since absolute focus is on what can be controlled — the now. Life no longer consists of looking *there*; because the focal point is now *here*. Life no longer is encumbered from the mind thinking about *tomorrow* or *yesterday*; therefore, the heart is aligned perfectly with *today*. Life is no longer burdened with *pain* and *suffering*; rather abundant with *peace of mind* and *joy*. The attention is no longer drawn toward the *wants* of life; rather appreciation is shown for the things one already does *have*. And certainly, life's purpose is no longer anchored to *becoming*; but entirely focused on *being*.

Isaac Newton, the legendary scientist of the late 1600s and early 1700s who recognized the concept of gravity, was unquestionably aware of the relationship between actions and reactions. In the mentioned phone call between my brother and me, Justin beautifully touched on the essence of Newton's third law: "Every action has an equal and opposite reaction."[2] It is imperative for the conscious reaction to be one of positivity rather than negativity. A positive outlook is the direct portal to an enlightened state of living. Whereas a negative mindset is sure to be a fast track to the gates of Hell. The choice of positive reaction is one that needs to be made each and every moment. Yes, I realize it is initially fairly difficult to maintain this type of positive consciousness always, but with confidence, persistence, and practice it increasingly becomes second nature.

As we will see shortly, Justin has the keen ability to frequently abide in this positive, blissful realm regardless of the situation at hand. No matter what curveballs of life are thrown at us, our outer, external state is always a direct reflection to our inner state of existence and consciousness. If we are self-confident and positive on the inside, our outer world almost magically transforms into a place of beauty, peace, and fruitfulness. Contrarily, if our inner state is negative and doubting, negativity and inadequate results will be the outcome.

Precisely stated, our perception determines our reality. What we are looking for in life is usually what we'll find. It is like when flipping through the pages of a *Where's Waldo?* picture book. On a single page, there is a countless number of faces illustrated, but only one is truly noticeable and seen—the face of Waldo. Similarly, in life there is an infinite number of possible reactions to any given scenario—and when we choose to find the positivity and seed of opportunity in whatever we encounter—positivity, opportunity, and plentitude are what will manifest as the result.

Another relative, yet looser comparison when dissecting the above phrase is similar to when somebody purchases a new car. For all intents and purposes, let's say the car's color is yellow. I guarantee the first couple of weeks after buying the car, he/she will notice more yellow cars than ever before on the road. It is not likely that everyone else in the community actually went to the dealership the same day and bought a yellow car. Rather, the influx of yellow cars seen is because the individual is now consciously aware of his/her own vehicle's color scheme, which reflects and translates to recognizing more yellow cars in the external world on the highway.

When it all boils down to it, if you wake up knowing you are going to have a good day, I guarantee you will, in fact, have a good day. On the contrary, if you wake up thinking the day ahead will be bad, that is exactly how the day will unfold. All things considered, a positive perception is undoubtedly key regarding the actualization of complete self-confidence, and also overcoming adversity via persistence. Just remember that in each and every moment the outer world is directly reflecting and correlating to your inner state. By being aware of this, you will be sure to never stray too far from the present moment.

In the following sections, we will delve deep into Justin's history and depict how he is a symbol of the above characteristics described. To bring the introductory portion of the current chapter to a close, I want to wrap up this section with a quote from the impactful and insightful Napoleon Hill, an American self-help author of the 1900s. He is most commonly known for his book titled *Think and Grow Rich*, which is among the top ten best-selling self-help books of all time. In another one of his books, *Outwitting the Devil: The Secret to Freedom and Success*, Hill "digs deep to identify the greatest obstacles we face in reaching our personal goals—including fear, procrastination, anger and jealousy—as tools orchestrated by the Devil himself."[3] Throughout the book, Hill describes his question and answer-like conversation with the imaginary, yet real, Devil inside his head. As a result, he simplifies answers to life's most complicated questions and provides solutions on how to go around some of our most burdensome, self-imposed obstacles. I shall end this portion with Napoleon Hill's written words from inside the front cover of *Outwitting the Devil*, which in a roundabout way sums up the contents of this introduction:

Fear is the tool of the man-made devil. Self-confident faith in one's self is both the man-made weapon which defeats this devil and the man-made tool which builds a triumphant life. And it is more than that. It is a link to the irresistible forces of the Universe which stand behind a man who does not believe in failure and defeat as being anything but temporary experiences.[4]

Justin's Surprising News

As with all of us, Justin has experienced many ups and downs throughout his life. Often times, many of the so-called downs in life originate from a place not within an individual's sphere of control. When an uncontrollable event or situation materializes, there are two ways to respond. One reaction is to negatively complain about whatever happened or is happening. The other reaction consists of the opposite side of the coin and is one of positive acceptance. Even though the situation doesn't make the person happy, he/she is aware that there is a way out or around the obstacle existing immediately at the forefront. Complaining about something that already happened doesn't serve justice to anyone. It is pointless and a waste of energy. The event has been decided, and the only thing in one's control is the reaction to said event. At that point, relative to the first type of response mentioned above, usually the unfortunate event will snowball downward. Things will spiral out of control and perhaps breed and attract an increasing number of undesirable events—ultimately leading to more negative reactions—then continuing with the negative action/reaction sequence on autoloop. Whereas on the other hand, a positive reaction of acceptance results in a world of difference. The undesirable event—although still not bringing direct joy or happiness—is met with a contrasting perspective. The person who positively reacts possesses an elevated level of confidence, certain that the current temporary adversity will be conquered. He/she realizes that the way in which his/her reaction transpires determines how, why, and when the situation will subside. On top of that, when the transient event passes, a valuable lesson is usually learned by the positive reactor to carry moving forward.

Detrimental situations and occurrences are bound to happen in the midst of life. Nobody skirts through unscathed. At any rate, the events are not what signify a person. Instead, the way in which the individual reacts is the defining factor of character. Justin experienced one of these uncontrollable examples of adversity when he was in 8th grade.

In Chapter 2, 8th grade Justin was discussed briefly. We already know he was the vice president of his middle school class, but that's as far as we went. Justin was an exception to the "Jack of all trades, master of none" saying. A relative phrase that closer suited Justin's reality would be "Jack of all trades, master of all." By no means was Justin a master of all trades yet, but stacked on top of his impressive accolades in the classroom and innate ability to not take life too seriously—always saving room for a well-timed joke—Justin actively played for the middle school football and ice hockey teams. He always rose to the occasion no matter how busy his schedule was. Some evenings, since

THE 2650 MILE AISLE

the seasons crossed over, Justin would promptly attend football practice following school and then go straight to his hockey practice, sometimes getting dressed in the car on the way so he was not late. Every aspect of Justin's life was aligned how he planned it; good grades, a supportive group of friends, and he was a part of winning sports teams. It seemed as if not a single force in the world was able to dethrone him from his crown.

That is until the chariots of life took a sharp left turn during his 8th grade sports physical examination. Sports physicals are an annual occurrence for student athletes and are normally rather procedural, with the student athlete in and out in less than ten minutes. The doctors and trainers measure heights, weights, body fat percentages, test reflexes, and last but certainly not least, require a urine sample from the student. That one sunny summer morning at roughly 8:30 AM was when Justin's life would change forever. Justin—always staying relatively healthy as a lifelong athlete—breezed by the first segments of the physical with flying colors. Then, his last checkpoint before he was free to go enjoy the beautiful day by soaking in a refreshing wave pool or hooting and hollering at a cookout with his buddies—was urinating in a cup. The doctor handed Justin the cup to privately urinate behind the sliding cloth he closed behind him. Without hesitation, Justin filled the container as requested and returned it to the doctor. The doctors at physical examinations execute an initial, basic test of the student's urine for an assortment of different diseases to ensure it does not need to be sent to a lab for further testing. After the initial inspection, I recall Justin saying his doctor's face screamed with uneasiness. The doctor explained to my brother that his urine sample was going to be sent to a hospital and that he should not participate in sports practice the remainder of the week for safety purposes. As prudent doctors commonly exhibit, he refused to determine an exact prognosis for Justin until the test results were received.

    Later that day, the school nurse called our home phone and left a voice recording on the message machine. She said that Justin or my parents needed to call the school as soon as possible upon receiving the message. My family and I sensed the discomfort in her voice as she murmured the notification, holding back tears with her broken words. Justin perused through the family contact list in our kitchen and assertively dialed up the school's phone number. We all anxiously waited in the adjacent room for what felt like a millennium, thinking of the worst-case scenario. We heard the click of Justin hanging up the phone and rushed to his side, flooding him with questions only loving family members would ask. 8th grade Justin calmed us down and explained how the school believed he had type 1 diabetes, and how he should go to Children's Hospital immediately to confirm the results and start taking the next steps.

THE 2650 MILE AISLE

The test results remained consistent. Justin was, in fact, officially diagnosed with type 1 diabetes.

My family and I spent a majority of the next week in and out of the hospital Justin was being cared for in. The nurses provided Justin with an overwhelming amount of information regarding the disease: what he should eat, how to test his blood sugar, how to take insulin shots, what his future would look like, as well as dangers and risks inherent with diabetes, among a multitude of other topics. A typical 8th grader would have broken down in tears halfway through the nurse's informed lecturing. When hearing the potential of going blind later in life, or the reality of being required to prick fingers to test blood sugar levels at least five times a day—a standard middle schooler would have pouted and complained about how their newly discovered disease wasn't fair.

But Justin was not in the least the average 8th grader. Although not jumping with joy, he fully accepted the type 1 diabetes diagnosis and was grateful they recognized it early on at his athletic physical examination instead of months or years down the road. Justin completely acknowledged the fact that he would retain the disease his entire life, but he almost viewed it as a test. By accepting the situation at hand, Justin reckoned it the opportunity for him to ascend beyond the petty roadblock and progress and grow as a human being out of the situation.

I distinctly remember clear as day the one specific visit my family and I had with Justin. It was earlier in the week of his diagnosis and a nurse was still bedside monitoring Justin's vitals. We huddled together in the room and earnestly listened to the nurse as she spoke her technical jargon relating to the disease, and also the 'user-friendly' version of what everything she was saying meant for Justin. She respected our privacy and gave Justin and us some time together while she fetched his lunch. As she gently closed the door behind her, panic amongst my family erupted in the hospital room. Just a few of the questions my family posed: "What type of food are we going to need?" "How will Justin be able to go to school?" "Will this affect his plan to play sports in high school?" In my family's defense, the mayhem was warranted as type 1 diabetes is extremely serious and nobody in our family ever lived with the disease, so we were all—especially Justin—diving into unknown waters. The serious discussion continued for a few more moments.

At that point, I remember glancing over at Justin to see what his take was on all of this. He was calmly resting upright in the hospital bed, delicately scanning the room around him, with the slightest of grins painted to his face. Ironically, he appeared to be the least concerned individual in the room. Moreover, he added insight and a dash of composure to the family conversation with his non-emotional conjectures. Justin sat there cool as the

THE 2650 MILE AISLE

other side of his hospital bed pillow, without an ounce of worry in his eyes or invisible weight on his shoulders. A few minutes passed and in a relaxed, matter-of-fact manner Justin mentioned he needed to prick his finger before his meal to record his blood sugar levels. Shortly after, his nurse returned to the room carrying a plate of a scrumptious looking turkey wrap, and fresh smelling sweet potato fries, paired with a cup of chunky applesauce. The nurse reminded Justin that before he started to eat he would need to test his blood sugar. He motioned to the written number on the clipboard on his bed and a rather surprised but proud smile shaped on nurse's face.

Type 1 diabetes was not Justin's choice. Nor was it desirable for him to be given the diagnosis when in 8th grade. And certainly, Justin's input was not taken into consideration in this situation. But 8th grade Justin realized all of these things. He also was aware of the only thing in his control in relation to the irreversible disease; his reaction. Justin accepted the diabetes in stride. From the initial prognosis in the gymnasium up until today, he has remained unphased by type 1 diabetes. Justin transformed a boulder of an obstacle into a hardly existing pebble on the road that he travels. A considerable bulk of his overcoming of adversity, and the act of diminishing its power, is accredited to the positive mindset and sureness of self he possessed throughout the entire process—even when he laid in that hospital bed peacefully in control after having been diagnosed with type 1 diabetes many summers ago.

His Body is a Temple

Justin, along with his high school football teammates, were granted the privilege of gaining access to the weight room whenever they chose throughout the season. The coaches were even kind enough to give them the key for a few months before the games started as well. This meant Justin had unlimited access to a gym for approximately six months out of the year. When Justin started onto a specific workout regimen, good luck trying to stop or hinder the freight train that was chugging full force down its track. Once Justin planned out the times and days he would work out in the gym—nothing, and I mean absolutely nothing—would deter him from following through one way or another. I recall that he prioritized working out during the season and would sacrifice his time participating in less important activities. As committed as he was in the gym, he still managed to live a balanced life in high school. Instead of going to the party that started at 7:30, after pumping some iron to prepare for the season, he would show up around 9 o'clock and enjoy his evening. The way in which he balanced his time and energy was like watching a plate-spinning act at the Cirque du Soleil. As determined as he was to complete whatever activity he placed in front of himself, once his workout was finished, the thought of the gym would not cross his mind until the next time he was there. He realized that doing so would be a waste of energy and focus so he alternatively vested his energy towards the present moment.

During the season, he appeared to be lifting weights and working out for the sole purpose of increasing his performance on the playing field. It wasn't until after the football season that I realized enhancing his abilities and endurance was only one aspect of the reason why he worked out as relentlessly as he did. There was a deeper, more meaningful reason below the surface. After his football season concluded, Justin and my older sister purchased a membership to the gym located a few miles away. Both Alexa, who played soccer, and my brother—who was in the midst of his hockey season—juggled busy schedules and were hard-pressed for available times to attend the gym together. Rather than banishing the gym membership, they arrived at a solution. Every weekday before school they drove in the pitch dark to workout at the bare gym. Waking up at 4:30 in the morning in high school is not the ideal approach to senior year. But like day follows night, Justin and Alexa exercised at the gym up the street before school each and every day. They set this precedence for themselves at the onset of their choice and treated it as a sacred practice of sorts—never once skipping out to sleep in a warm, comfortable bed for a couple more hours.

Justin was the opposite of vain, and he never flexed his muscles in the mirror, asked if he looked good, or even made a remark that insinuated he cared how other people superficially viewed him. After having the honor of observing Justin my entire life, I reached the conclusion there was a more precious, intangible basis for why he cared for his body—almost religiously. Only foods and activities that were beneficial to his well-being were digested and enjoyed by him. He treated calories as fuel and deduced each one to be as efficient as possible for his ultimate health and energy, although still saving room for a piece of chocolate cake from time to time. This correlated translation of a disciplined, balanced diet and lifestyle is one that carried over into the gym. He respected his body to such a high order that if he had not increased his blood flow and circulation of oxygen by working out, he would deem it as a disservice to himself. Emotionally, it is easy for a human being to succumb to the temptation of regularly eating deliciously greasy, yet unhealthy food—and refusing to jump out of bed to go to the gym on a chilly, tired morning. But Justin was in control of his emotions, like a pilot flying a plane across the country. His objective vantage point toward himself allowed him to say "No" to the can of soda and say "Yes" to the gym at 4:30 on a sub-zero Monday morning mid-February. Simply deduced, I've realized that Justin did—and still does to this day—treat his body like a temple.

CAMERON JAMES WILLIAMS

The Blemish Never Seen

Although Justin has always treated his body as if it were a temple, it didn't deter the inevitability of an extra secretion of facial oils when transforming from a boy to man amid puberty. The natural process of puberty results in a laundry list of unavoidable bodily changes such as: a deeper voice, growth of underarm hair, and most commonly feared by teenagers—acne. Some people never fall victim to the perceived curse of an increasing number of pimples, and others—no matter how much one washes his/her face—aren't as fortunate and end up resembling a pepperoni pizza when all is said and done. In high school, Justin inescapably joined the latter of these two groupings. But instead of curling up in a ball of anxiety and worrying about having acne on his face, he shamelessly faced the situation at hand head-on.

"Because one believes in oneself, one doesn't try to convince others. Because one is content with oneself, one doesn't need others' approval. Because one accepts oneself, the whole world accepts him or her."[1] This is a powerful quote from Lao Tzu, the famous ancient Chinese philosopher and founder of philosophical Taoism. His words translate seamlessly to Justin's encounter with acne throughout high school. Justin was fully aware that he was unable to control his hormones at the onset of pubescence, so what did he do as a result? He completely accepted the reality of the situation and viewed it as a test of his self-confidence. Even as a teen, Justin knew his outer appearance was only a drop of water in the overflowing bucket of who he truly was. As simple as it sounds, he remained unaffected by acne because he didn't let acne affect him. This point relates back to the fact of life that our reactions to events that happen are the only things we are able to truly control. The actuality of his high school life was that acne was a part of his developmental process.

To this truth that was set in stone, he had two possible responses. One was a response of negativity. The negative response would have weighed on his subconscious and deflated the fulfillment of his own goals as well as hinder the interactions amongst his peers. The end result of this negativity would be the destruction of self confidence and paralyzing of progression of character growth due to fear—becoming frozen in time like woolly mammoth's skeleton during the ice age. The other path of response—the one Justin traveled—was a positive response. This latter reaction was one of acceptance, courage, and confidence. It's a response of recognizing the control in one's power. Justin realized that dwelling on the blemishes on his face would only make matters worse, as how we feel on the inside radiates outwards to our external world. His positive feeling of wholeness on the inside—regardless of how he looked on the outside—transmitted light to his external world. As a result, even the cruelest of kids in the school accepted and respected Justin for who he actually was. Nobody ever drew attention to his acne because, frankly, I think everyone couldn't help but see past it. The reason for this is because Justin took the initiative to confidently accept and respect himself for the person he was first, and the following response was reciprocated exactly in his outer world.

I sometimes reflect back on those times when he was in high school, pondering if he was actually as steadfast as he appeared regarding his acne. The pessimistic side of me tends to think deep down the pimples on his face issued some sort of negative effect on his self-confidence. But then after concentrating deeper into the situation, I arrive at the realization that the type of immovable demeanor he displayed was not one that can be emulated. He never showed that his experience with acne bothered him—because genuinely I believe it never did, in fact, alter his disposition—as even a trace of his uneasiness would have been emitted externally and have become noticeable. The unruffling of his metaphoric teenage feathers proved that he passed that specific test with flying colors. Ultimately, Justin's clash with acne in high school bred an increased sense of self-confidence as well as a 'leveling up' of his true inner character in general. He innately was cognizant of the fact that the analogous storm would eventually run out of rain, and the skies—as well as his face—would clear up.

But representative to his nature, Justin would cross that bridge when he came to it. For that time being, his utmost focus was on his current step—not the road ahead nor the road behind. If he was aware of Abraham Lincoln's legendary utterance or not I do not know, but a teenage Justin incontestably embodied his timeless statement, "And this too, shall pass away."[2] Those six words penetrate deeply across all aspects of life—whether good, bad, and everything in between. Abraham Lincoln, as well as Justin, were certain that every blemish in life was sure to fade.

The Unsung Hero

Everything in life is temporary. Justin's high school football career was no exception to this. Justin's career extended into college, but that's the extent of which we will discuss his college career at this time. As previously mentioned, Justin was a defensive as well as offensive lineman for his football team. In the area of western Pennsylvania where we grew up, high school football was treated like a religion. As a ritualistic practice, most of the community would jam-pack the stadiums on Friday nights (even if only standing room was available) to watch their local team duke it out against a neighboring school district. Looking back, it is almost unbelievable how serious high school football was perceived by not just the players—but the entire community. But in any case, that was the nature of it, so Justin accepted the sacred duty proudly, for his local township and himself—but more so for the sake of doing it justly. In his senior year, Justin's team impressively finished the regular season undefeated, receiving a great deal of publicity from the local news stations and journalists. The public exposure was ironic because Justin never desired to be in the limelight. If I recall, he found the concept rather foolish.

On top of that, each Friday in school, decorative and exuberant pep rallies were a normality to boost the team's morale. And then later that night in a matter-of-fact manner, Justin approached each game professionally and went out on the field to take care of business over the course of four quarters. After the game, he left the locker room satisfied but never got too high on the highs. And I would conclude that if he ever were to lose he wouldn't have gotten too low on the lows either. As we now have a better understanding of high school football in the region we lived, let us proceed to the focal point of the current section; Justin's senior football banquet.

At the banquet, sparks flittered and emotions skyrocketed for his teammates, as it would more than likely be the last official congregation they would share together. I remember Justin came close to shedding a tear, believe or not, as the bond between his teammates and him became incredibly solidified over the prior four years. But for the majority of the emotional presentation, Justin calmly sat next to his poignant teammates—resembling his unmoved self in the hospital bed in 8th grade after being diagnosed with diabetes. Now I know it sounds like Justin is an emotionless potato at times, but he is far from that. He oozes with emotion and passion in everything he undertakes—but the difference is he has the unique ability to have the utmost control of his emotions—and is able to use them for his benefit rather than to his demise. He feels as all human beings feel, except he holds authority over the feelings; not the other way around.

THE 2650 MILE AISLE

The banquet initially commenced with a wide assortment of delicious foods offered in a buffet-like arrangement. From chicken and beef brisket, to green beans and mashed potatoes—you name it—this banquet host served it. After the meal, with the guests' bellies filled to maximum capacity, the coaches took the floor. The assistant coaches gave their thanks and kind regards to the seniors who were graduating that year. After three or four nearly identical sermon-esque addresses, the head coach of the football team stood front and center, ready to provide his long-winded and heartfelt deliverance. He plucked the emotional chords of the audience, which consisted of the players and their family members, by reminiscing on the season and rehashing some of the fondest memories of the year. As to be expected, mentions of brotherhood and perseverance were highlighted.

But the specific final remarks of the head coach's speech were not as anticipated. He didn't conclude his speech commending the running back of the team who finished with the most yards in the league; or the five-plus students who were to play at a Division 1 school the following year; or even hyping up the next season to carry the winning tradition onward. He chose to trot a different route to the finish line. He decided to single out one of the team captains to applaud him. He attested to this individual's determination. He spoke of his unparalleled work ethic. He acclaimed how his captain entered the locker room and left the field the same exact way; with a smile. He noted how this young man silently led the team from the bottom, only vocalizing when necessary; but when he did every single player listened. He emphasized on the fact that this player let his actions do his talking. And last but not least the head coach's final words were calling this player the unsung hero of the undefeated team. Do you have any guess who this player was?

In sum, choosing "The Only Way is Through" as the title of this chapter was a no-brainer. Throughout the chapter, we have learned how adversity is inevitable in life. Nothing great in this world was ever achieved without obstacles and temporary failures along the way. What's indicative of the external perspective of an individual being great is not the hardships one has faced—but how he/she reacted to the difficulties experienced. Did the person quiver in fear and submit all hope to the misfortune? Or was the challenge met directly with positivity and the certainty that there is a way to the other side—and that the obstacle is merely a bump in the road? An individual's response to the above questions determines a night and day difference in not only the person's character, but also the resulting effect thereafter. Did the person give up? Or did he/she dig deeper within themselves and display an unwavering persistence? Was the individual worrying about every possible scenario that could go wrong? Or was there a laser focus on the controllable actions that could be taken in the present moment? The answers to these questions establish if somebody is a coward or a hero.

Failure is only permanent if it is accepted as so. For someone who has an inexorable self-confidence and a positive mindset to overcome any and all adversity in life —failure is non-existent. The word is not even in his/her vocabulary. The conscious choice between either tireless persistence or failure is the separating factor in any endeavor. The following illustration is a prime example of this significant choice. Napoleon Hill, in his book *Three Feet from Gold: Turn Your Obstacles into Opportunities!*,[1] presents an outstanding business allegory about a young man who chose the latter path of failure during the years of the gold rush. After mining away at a Colorado gold mine for many months, the gentleman quit. It was discovered later on that when the gentleman gave up, he was only three feet away from gold. Three. Measly. Feet. Keep this story in mind next time you think all odds are stacked against you when on the hinge of deciding defeat instead of perseverance.

Justin has proven over the years—as we have seen from only a few examples—that he is aware of the requirements and true meaning of greatness. Through even the most difficult of situations encountered—such as his diabetes diagnosis in middle school—he has remained unaffected. And on top of that, he has risen to the occasion against any form of adversity—substantial or paltry—and never cowardly succumbed to it. The reason being is that his belief in himself outweighed any sort of doubt; his positive attitude trumped any form of negativity; and his willingness to push forward eclipsed any thought of remaining stagnant. Throughout any challenge, Justin was and still is certain of two things. The first is of the thing he can control; his reaction. And the second is possessing the absolute certainty that there is a way through to the other side. Positivity is unquestionably a key ingredient in both of these truths as well. By remaining in the present moment constantly—not looking at the miles of road ahead or in the rearview mirror behind—every opposition suddenly became manageable and Justin was capable of reacting accordingly.

The majority of people are familiar with the glass half empty or glass half full idea. With that being said, knowing what this phrase means is one thing but embodying its essence is a completely contrasting story. Justin, from my observation and experience of being his brother, has ceaselessly kept his cup filled. I've concluded that a major contributing element to his optimistic outlook is his self-confidence and faith in himself. Michelangelo, arguably one of the greatest artists of all time, once squarely stated "Faith in oneself is the best and safest course."[2] Now, I'm sure Michelangelo engaged many struggles throughout his life and career—but his belief in himself aided in the conquering of his challenges. Another one of the most creative geniuses of all time, Vincent van Gogh, also touched on this point tastefully when proclaiming, "Painting is a faith, and it imposes the duty to disregard public opinion."[3] It is obviously clear throughout history, today, and surely to be true in the future, that when an individual surpasses any adversity in life—it is because his/her belief in him/herself outweighs the belief or lack thereof from anybody else. This statement is true with Michelangelo; van Gogh; Steve Jobs; the Founding Fathers; Horatius; and last but not least, Justin, among an extensive list of others. All of these people share one thing in common when faced with an obstacle in life: each one is cognizant of the verity that the only way is through.

CAMERON JAMES WILLIAMS

CHAPTER 5: NEW BEGINNINGS

Here and now not only starts a new chapter of *The 2650 Mile Aisle* but also a new chapter in Justin's life. The previous analogous and literal chapters highlighted and consisted of his years in high school as well as further back into childhood. Although Justin's mental aptitude matured beyond his years, he was not officially dubbed a man until he turned eighteen, just days after he walked across the stage in a cap and gown. In his formal becoming of a man, the boy portion of his life came to a closure, but in turn, another door gaped open. Justin's new door he chose to walk through was to play Division 3 football at Case Western University and study engineering, a prestigious destination for his desired field. The reputation he so sturdily built up in his childhood and during high school mattered not anymore. His new beginnings were like pressing the restart button on a computer, but instead of his work being saved he must begin anew. A daunting challenge for many, but Justin—as expected—rose to the occasion equipped to the maximum degree. With the commencement of chartering foreign territory, he leveled up not only in the world of material achievements but also through intangible personal growth—which was arguably of greater significance to him. The material achievements arrived as a byproduct of his inner progression; not the other way around.

At college, Justin—although a relatively big fish in a moderate-sized pond in high school—was now swimming in a much larger body of water akin to one of the Great Lakes. There were now considerably more sizeable fish in the ecosystem he occupied. Some of these fish traveled from all over the world to congregate in this selective pool. It was quite literally time for Justin to sink or swim. The noble status Justin earned in the previous eighteen years was irrelevant at that point. When he flew away from the nest I was eager to see if he would replicate a similar commanding of respect and honor that he gracefully received in high school. By spreading his immense wings, he exceeded all expectations as we will witness throughout "New Beginnings."

As I reflect today, it was foolish to even contemplate if Justin would continue to push the perpetual limits of life or not. By ascending above one level, it meant there was an opportunity for him to press the envelope even further and surpass yet another segment—and so on and so forth. A fourteen-year-old Justin was aware of the certitude of this ongoing process; assuredly an eighteen-year-old Justin was just as alert of this truth, and perhaps more so. But simply because Justin possessed this rather esoteric knowledge, it did not alter the fact that it would still be a difficult task expressing it via action. Justin viewed the window of opportunity as a chance to refine his character and skills—ultimately progressing his life's purpose further. To him, higher-level education was merely another step in the road of the grand highway. Although classifying school as imperative, Justin's outlook on life penetrated eminently deeper than a degree. Acquiring a degree in engineering was the task at hand, so he pursued it wholeheartedly, but in the back of his mind, he was conscious that the piece of paper was only a minuscule aspect of life's fruitfulness.

Justin controls the unique ability to not become overwhelmed by any grenade thrown at him in life. A large part of how he executes this steadfastness is complimentary of him remaining one with the present moment at all times. The remaining portion of his unflappability is due to his capacity to persistently honor his fun-loving nature in anything he undertakes. Paradoxically, even in participation of the most deemed serious of tasks, Justin's lack of tension and worry allows him to accomplish the goal at hand successfully and most efficiently. But as unshakeable as his focus is when pursuing a so-called serious task, he always reserves room to crack a joke or slice the tension in the room. His precise judgment and consistent maintenance of equilibrium between knowing when to work and when to play is second to none.

Justin's lucidness and lighthearted outlook towards life can be described many different ways. But similar to how all streams eventually end up at the ocean, no matter which way his character is explained, the underlying seed of truth remains constant throughout. Famous quotes and sayings are solely a signpost for the profound meanings they symbolize. Justin supersedes speaking these inspirational words and dives straight into living in the essence of the hieroglyphs. With that being said, Mark Twain, the prominent American author, touched on Justin's mannerisms in life when he said, "Twenty years from now you will be more disappointed by the things that you didn't do than the ones you did do. So throw off the bowlines. Sail away from the safe harbor. Catch the trade winds in your sails. Explore. Dream. Discover."[1] The idiosyncratic parity of Justin's careless and careful character is elegantly depicted therein by Twain.

In this chapter, our quest will continue to unveil where the source of Justin's free-spirited nature and willingness to push every limit in life derives from. "New Beginnings" will streamline the transition between "Part 1: Pre-Miranda," and "Part 2: Post-Miranda." Upon completion of Part 1, Miranda will be more comprehensively revealed, and we will learn how their eerily similar personalities enhance each other to epic proportions. But for now, our focus is maintained on the final stretch of Justin's lone wolf chunk of his life. Case Western is the place where Justin proceeded to make leaps and bounds regarding his knack of: obtaining respect and honor from others; pushing any self-imposed limits to a greater extent—expanding his horizon vastly; and continuing to conquer the inevitable adversity faced in life. Furthermore, I'm sure Justin was positive the battle of his next level was won before it even started. Because of this, he welcomed the new beginnings approaching his life with arms wide open.

Halloweekend

Case Western is located only a few hours away from the house in Pittsburgh where Justin and I grew up. Because of this, my family and I attended almost every—if not every—football game at the home field Justin's freshman year. After the games, we would find a delicious local 'ma and pa' type restaurant that Justin recommended. After sitting down for an hour or two, enjoying tasty food and even better conversation, we would depart back to Pittsburgh.

Swamped with schoolwork during the week, the only time Justin went out with friends to party—and same with really anyone else at the university—was the weekends. The dedicated students at the school maintained a balanced school to party ratio. With the advanced level criteria and workload, the students at Case Western attended the school to study and party only if there was time; not the other way around. By necessity of excelling in the classroom, Justin followed suit with his teammates and fellow students in that aspect. With that being said, there wasn't a shortage of an extreme good time when the students did agree to let loose.

During Justin's freshman year, he chose to live in a dormitory with a Pittsburgh native and fellow lineman on the football team. Justin's only correspondence with the guy prior to meeting him was via telephone, but he was confident enough to share a room with him for a couple semesters. They hit it off immediately as they held many common interests with one another. Their freshmen years ended so splendidly that both of them joined the same fraternity the following year. It was an unwritten rule at Case Western that the football players joined this specific fraternity once eligible. I believe something like 80-85% of the house consisted of football players, while the other 15-20% of individuals were student athletes from other sports at the school.

  Often times in new situations in life, individuals attempt to create a facade of themselves that is a shift and alteration from their actual personality. Usually, this type of pretentiousness is transparent and the effect for the individual is opposite of the initial intention. In many instances, the person chooses this artificial route because there is a lack of self-confidence or unhappiness deep within. But ironically, when external judgments aren't a motive in a relationship, more attractive, meaningful connections arise—and certainly more genuine and long-lasting ones. In Justin's new situation of college, he decided to venture the latter path. He remained true to himself and never pretended to be something or somebody else. The way he talked to and treated his professors was the same way he treated his teammates. And the respect he gave to his befriended classmates was the exact same respect he gave to a student that he had never seen passing him on the sidewalk on the way to class. Ultimately, because of this—although not his reason for doing so—more friends and close bonds magnetized towards Justin than he could ever imagine. He was simply being himself, but that attracted his peers and professors like a cup of hot chocolate after a long day of sled riding.

It should come to no surprise that the mentioned type of immediate harmony manifested itself in the fraternity house too during Justin's sophomore year. After two days of living in the house, it was as if Justin and his fraternity brothers had known each other and been living together for two years. Within days there was a constant stream of delicious meals being cooked; footballs being thrown; pranks being played; and last but not least, perverted jokes being said throughout the household. All of this after they laboriously studied obviously. Justin—although new and unaccomplished in anyone else's eyes in the house—fit in immediately just by being himself. Within weeks of showing his talent in the kitchen, he gracefully received the honor of head chef. Without prior information given about the esteemed school or guys in his house, one would never guess in a million years that everyone in Justin's fraternity ranked toward the upper portion of their graduating classes in high school. And one would absolutely never predict that each and every one of the individuals would proceed to graduate

THE 2650 MILE AISLE

from Case Western the following years. These men—including Justin—were well aware that there was a time for work, but they absolutely were sure there was a time for play too. I was granted the privilege of witnessing and experiencing for myself all of the above, and then some, Justin's sophomore year when I visited him for Halloween weekend.

Sixteen or seventeen at the time, I had never experienced the college scene in general—let alone a college party with a fraternity. I didn't have an inkling of a clue of what to expect. After Justin's afternoon football game, my mom, dad, Abbey, and Alexa went their own way for the night, while I went with my brother. On the walk back to his place, I envisioned creeping into a room full of grizzled men who kept to themselves and were not enthused about visitors. Upon opening the door—to my pleasant surprise—exactly the opposite was the case (except the part about the grizzled men). It felt like a family reunion as I think at least half of the house introduced themselves to me within the first three minutes of entering the dwelling. Before Justin and I even navigated to his bedroom to settle in, I was already dubbed the nickname 'Little Justin' (being roughly 5'8" I will admit I do replicate a miniature version of my 6'1" older brother, so the name was rather fitting). We placed our bags in his room and then my tour guide continued the tour throughout the remainder of his residence. Aware that I was still slightly nervous—even after the grand welcoming which certainly washed away most of the nerves—Justin first acquainted me with the remaining members of the house that were jamming in one last hour of study time before the night of carousing was underway. At the doors that were shut, he playfully knocked on them—making up some sort of secret knock cadence or impersonating (alarmingly well) a woman's voice—to ease the interruption of concentration when introducing them to me. After hearing it was Justin, every single person opened their doors with smiles on their faces.

    Now that I was familiarized with everyone in the house, the next stint on our mini-excursion was the kitchen. This was not your average kitchen. In fact, this commercial kitchen may have been the largest room in the whole house. With a massive icebox, a cooking surface the size of Texas, and a pantry that I thought was going to lead to Narnia, some restaurants would have been jealous of the intricacies of this fraternity's behemoth kitchen. Halfway through the tour of the kitchen, Justin and I reunited with the group of gentlemen who originally greeted us. The one obvious prankster of the house who always wore a somewhat suspicious yet liberating smirk on his face grabbed a handful of chocolate chips and reared back to chuck them at me. Instead of immediately releasing them in my direction, he stood there frozen holding them like a present-day statue of one of the Minutemen clutching his musket during the Battle of Lexington and Concord in the late 1700s. And like one of

THE 2650 MILE AISLE

George Washington's soldiers in the Revolutionary War, he waited for his commander's permission to fire. Upon my brother's nod of approval, deliciously semi-melted chocolate chips rained down on me. No harm, no foul. I was mentally prepared for some sort of official initiation anyways (I mean it was a college fraternity, right?). That was a drop in a bucket compared to some of the fun-loving, yet extremely competitive battles Justin and I have endured against each other throughout our lives. As we grew older and more mature, I was increasingly more grateful that Justin aided in my mental preparation of facing hardships in life.

Justin and I looped back to the final stop on our tour—the starting point where we entered—before returning back to his room to prepare our Halloween costumes for the night ahead. Some of the guys were still watching the television. Others were immersed in a video game. And the same four guys who were grabbing a snack in the kitchen continued to toss a pigskin around the room like they were outside on the turf. As intelligent as these men were, they found excitement in throwing the football past objects in the room, coming as close as possible without breaking them. I did not ascertain this definitively, but I have a gut feeling that the prankster with the chocolate chips in the kitchen was the one who invented the game. With the official entrance tour complete, Justin and I simultaneously sat down on the couch to peek what game was on television. Some of his teammates were already beginning the Halloween celebration courtesy of spiked beverages. One of the respected veteran linemen on the team glanced our way and offered a drink to my brother. Justin gracefully accepted and told him that he owed him one. And then he asked for my brother's approval if it was okay to offer me a drink as well. My brother first turned my direction, and in an unintimidating and unbiased manner scanned me to see if I wanted to accept his kind gesture—and verbally assured there was no pressure and that the decision was completely mine.

    After a few more minutes of relaxing on the couch, Justin and I eagerly assembled our outfits for the exciting night ahead. Justin's choice of character was the 'Sun Drop Soda Man' sported with a Sun Drop t-shirt and retro headband (college students don't have the funds for much more than that), and I played the role of a sexy kitty cat (at least I think I looked pretty sexy). Justin showed me a good time and a half as we bounced from party to party, ensuring I received a full scope of what life was like at his college. At every party we undertook, my kitty cat costume was welcomed with open arms. Part of this effervescent reception was because of my drop-dead gorgeous pasty thighs; and the other part was because they saw who I was with.

    As previously mentioned, Justin and I—being brothers—have had our fair share of bouts where one of us crosses a line and takes a supposed joke too far. In those essentially harmless situations, we both had short memories and always forgave each other quickly. But when serious matters were at hand, Justin continuously was there for my best interest. No matter where the location or what the situation—although he would never admit—Justin accepted the role of being a 'watchful protector' or 'invisible guardian' seriously. To him, he just thinks that is what it means to be an older brother. Whatever the case, he plays the part wholeheartedly and precisely. When visiting him at college, even in utterly foreign territory, he was still the same exact Justin I knew and loved. Evidently, he received the same amount of respect and honor as he had in his middle school and high school years—if not more. With a full heart, I can proudly say I will never forget that weekend until the day I pass. Throughout that one Halloweekend many years ago, it felt as if I was in first grade riding in the back of the bus with Justin all over again.

CAMERON JAMES WILLIAMS

Oh Captain, My Captain

All four years throughout Justin's college football career, he was designated as first-string by his coaches. Although the competition was increasingly more intense than in high school—and the athletes on his and the other teams were full-grown men rather than boys—he continued to excel on the field. But instead of lining up against 6'2" offensive lineman in high school, the normal stature of his opponent in college was nothing less than 6'5". On top of that, the seasoned offensive lineman weighed at least one hundred pounds more than they had years prior. Justin adapted accordingly and relied on his speed and agility rather than brute strength, which he realized would be a waste of labor and a pointless, endless battle not worth fighting. Because of his keen adaptations in playing style, Justin continued to impress both his teammates and coaches alike.

But Justin was never entirely concerned of the opinions of his coaches and teammates, as the opinions played a meager role in his achievements on the field. Furthermore, Justin was well aware that the opinions and judgments of others were elements that were not in his control. Instead, he focused on the things he was positive were in his capacity to control, such as his work ethic, his willingness to improve, and his character on and off the field. Evidently, when those three aspects were considered and realized wholeheartedly, the opinions and judgments sorted themselves out accordingly. To prove this, Justin was voted as one of the team captains his junior year. The selection of this honored position was voted solely by the players on the team. Receiving this responsibility was somewhat ironic for Justin—because being a captain of the team was never his sole motive—but his consistent actions and leadership on and off the field led him to this destiny. Granted, once he was selected, he accepted the dubbing with a sense of duty and determination. He never changed his character or let his ego become inflated, but he continued on the same noble course as he had before the votes. As in high school, Justin was never innately a vocal leader on the field or in the locker room. Nevertheless, leaders come in all shapes and sizes. Justin either consciously or naturally chose the path of leading by example. Justin inspired and motivated his teammates not with 'rah rah' speeches but by embodying the sacrifice and work ethic required to be a winner on and off the playing field. Now with that being said, when Justin did speak—everyone listened undoubtedly.

Justin's character remained consistent whether on the playing field, in the classroom, with his friends, or with his family. How Justin thinks and acts when alone in silence is exactly the same Justin seen and unveiled in the public light. He truly defies economist Timur Kuran's theory of Preference Falsification, as previously mentioned in the "The Williams Name" section of Chapter 2. Instead of the common characteristic throughout society of the prevalence of a Private Truth and Public Lie rationale—with respect to Justin—his private truth aligns harmoniously with his public truth. There aren't any inconsistencies or contrast between his internal thoughts and his external actions. That specific trait is an incredibly admirable one—yet extremely rare.

Justin's infectious confidence and sureness in himself is a thing of beauty to experience first-hand and witness when in relation to other people. Rather than wasting time attempting to prove himself to other people, he focuses on pushing the limits of himself and life in general. Two things are guaranteed when Justin undertakes a challenge: his entire energy and effort will be devoted and sacrificed to the overcoming of said challenge; and his utter confidence that the challenge will be trumped is present. Neither of the two guarantees he provides, or better yet anything Justin has ever accomplished in his life, would be possible if it wasn't for his ceaseless positive outlook and mentality towards life. His sustained positivity, in effect, leads to a never-ending spew of self-confidence from his fruitful, pure faucet that is his heart. Justin will always be perceived as a captain by others in life. Whether officially labeled by them or not—or if he is even aware of it or cares for that matter—he will continue to lead by example and inspire in life. At any rate, Justin's character is an unquestionable symbol of the meaning of the true essence of the word captain.

Fall Seven Times, Stand Up Eight

The famous proverb "Fall seven times, stand up eight"[1] encompasses a world of truth regarding adversity. It is rephrased or reworded across a multitude of religious, spiritual, motivational, and self-help texts. But living in the saying is the core of what perseverance accurately means. It reemphasizes the fact that failure is merely a temporary setback and is never permanent unless accepted as so. Determination and courage shine brightly through the six words. The actions and examples beneath the words exemplify and prove the saying true. In Justin's college football career, he illustrates the above quote precisely—having fallen victim to injuries among many other obstacles—but analogously and literally standing up every time he was knocked down.

During Justin's junior year at Case Western Reserve University, he suffered a season-ending injury. Due to the damage in his collarbone from a collision happening in a game, coaches and trainers deemed him unable to return to the playing field that year. The coaches spelled out to him clearly that he was not by any means required to attend the games the rest of the season, and that it would not be taken personally if he focused solely on his schoolwork instead. In typical Justin fashion, he was present on the sideline for every single game that remained in the season—both home and away.

Although he was standing on the sideline with a sling around his shoulder and neck, he was still determined to contribute to his team finishing victoriously each and every Saturday. His voluntary presence on the sidelines was motivational enough to his teammates, but Justin advanced a step farther. He accepted the role of being a composition of a scout, coach, player, and trainer. He pointed out anything he noticed from his perspective that would enhance his team's possibility of winning the game. Justin's attendance at the successive games was like having a twelfth man on the field. His commitment to his team, to himself, and to his role as captain as well, was immensely evident even in the contests he was unable to officially suit up for.

The next season, he returned to the field in tip-top condition ready to finish his college football career strong and on a high note. Being well-rested from the shortened season the year prior, he was chomping at the bit to reinstate his leading presence on the turf. Justin's team established their winning mentality immediately, starting the season with three wins and zero losses. Justin was an instrumental aspect of the team's success — leading his team in tackles up until that point.

Everything was going swimmingly until the fourth game of the Justin's senior season, when an opposing player fell on his leg the wrong way and injured his MCL. From an external perspective, it appeared that Justin could not catch a break and that would be the last time he ever stepped foot onto a football field. The trainers informed Justin that it was highly unlikely that he would return to the turf that year. Justin accepted the challenge and rehabilitated his knee almost religiously. Every single day that his team practiced, Justin was rehabbing his knee to increase strength and flexibility—slowly but surely reducing his recovery time. It goes without saying that Justin accompanied his team on the sideline and locker room each game he was on the IR. To his teammates, coaches, and trainers' pleasant surprise, Justin shortened his recovery time by a few weeks and was deemed healthy enough to play the final two games of the season—and his football career. Justin consistently played like it was his last time on the field every game prior in his career, and certainly he was not about to stop this type of tenacity in his actual last two games.

    Justin left his heart and soul on the football field those last two games. Although sad to watch in one sense, it was rather gratifying and humbling in another light knowing that he left nothing else in the tank—the last two games—and in his whole career in general. Justin, as to be expected, was emotional for a short stint after the final time on the football field but quickly regained his composure, because he was cognizant of the fact that he enjoyed every single moment while it happened. Justin was always well aware of the fact that the only permanent thing in this world is change itself.

THE 2650 MILE AISLE

He recognized deep within him that when one door closed another door was guaranteed to open in the constant ebb and flow of life. Anyone that is closely acquainted with Justin—whether a teammate, family member, fellow employee, and so on—can verify that Justin's courageous and resolute spirit is existent and observable in every one of his life's aspirations. Ultimately, one thing is undeniably true throughout any one of Justin's endeavors in his days on this planet: if he falls seven times, he will stand up eight.

CAMERON JAMES WILLIAMS

Something Old and Something New

Although at the time Justin was in the ring wrestling the larger opponent of an engineering degree in college, he never forgot about his past bouts and who was there for him in his corner. Every summer or winter vacation that Justin returned home to Pittsburgh, he reunited with his old high school friends and teammates. Whilst he was fond of everyone in his grade, he maintained a solid core of compadres throughout his teenage years. These were guys and gals that would take a bullet for Justin—as I'm sure he would return the favor if it came to that point. Their friendship signified what the essence of true friendship is. It wasn't a transactional friendship or a friendship by utility. Nobody kept a scoresheet of favors done for one another. No one in the group stealthily attempted to gain an advantageous upper hand. Those were not the type of people Justin chose to associate with. Rather, a friendship was prevalent for the sake of friendship itself; not for any hidden or underlying motive. Everyone in the group passed power back and forth to each other—perhaps exposing a form of vulnerability by doing this—but in totality it made the group and each individual within the group increasingly stronger and more powerful that way.

Often times—as many other so-called cliques that associated with each other in Justin's

THE 2650 MILE AISLE

high school proved—there was slowly a divorce and degradation of superficially perceived sound friendships. As years went on, these other friendships grew further and further apart. A change of interest or a change of heart—or a change of something which I am not exactly sure—was obvious as individuals seemed to tidily package up their past on a sailboat and send it off to sea. As these people banished their past lives, they were neck-deep in other relationships—perceived as better—with people they met in college a year or two previously. In the snap of a finger, many friendships disappeared, and not unusually so much so that former best friends couldn't even afford a phone call to one another. These (bluntly put) weak individuals were chasing something that they could never quite reach. The metaphoric grass was always greener on another lawn.

    Justin achieved the exact opposite with his group of high school friends. He managed to maintain the landscape of his older lawn while also tending to the vast acres of bountiful farmland he acquired in his college years. Justin managed to plant fields of agriculture and travel many miles of the immense plot's growth on his tractor in college—but when it was time to return to the barn it was like it was the only piece of land he ever owned—while still remaining conscientious of the immense swath of crop that was in his possession. While many contrary foolish individuals' outlooks thought the most convenient route to take was to send a new farmer out into the field to tend to their crops—treating the barn, its yard, and the farmland as separate pieces of land—Justin chose the opposite path. Justin's exact same analogous farmer who lived in the barn was also the farmer who was riding the tractor in the field. Rather than not knowing the outcome of how the grass was cut in the field or how aesthetically pleasing the vista was reckoned, Justin was unambiguously aware that all the estate was his own. There was no divide. Both plots of land were treated as one piece of property from Justin's vantage point.

    I vividly remember this above truth manifesting itself at my high school graduation afterparty. Everyone that remained at nightfall was hooting and hollering having an old-fashioned good time. One of the beer kegs was kicked. All the older folks had filtered their way out as the sun dropped into the horizon, and it was just the young bucks left. Obviously, my close friends were in attendance. But so were my older sister's friends and my brother's as well. Graduation parties within our family had become a sacred tradition of sorts—as there was two test-runs before mine—and each year they became more extravagant and elaborate, running later into the night each sequential year. As there was three years since Alexa's high school graduation party, mine was highly anticipated by not only my friends and family, but my older brother's friends as well.

THE 2650 MILE AISLE

The food burners were shut off, the greasy fried chicken was at room temperature, and flies started hovering over the clumped-up potato salad. That was a sign that the real party—the afterparty—had officially commenced as each individual that was daring enough to endure congregated in the garage. The next-door neighbors were already forewarned of the heightened noise levels that were to follow that evening—and a saran wrapped to-go variety plate of delectable cookies was sure to ascertain their cooperation of the pandemonium that was bound to ensue. As varying ages and groups of people packed like sardines in our expansive garage, good conversations and even better vibes began to circulate throughout the room.

Not only were Justin's high school friends in attendance, but a slew of his college friends who lived locally in the Pittsburgh region were invited as well—and they all showed up. An individual with varying identities would be sure to have been overflown with anxiety and worry in that sort of situation, in hopes that one group wouldn't blow the cover of his/her alter ego. He/she would have strenuously battled the uphill fight of trying to appease both the high school and college friends separately, while ultimately at the same time. Evidently, this nightmare of a situation would have carried on for an eternity and eventually end in a disaster—as undoubtedly one person cannot act as two people at the same time. This worst-case-scenario never even crossed Justin's mind, as the same guy he was in high school was the same guy he was in college (except maybe the college version was a little hairier and could drink more beer). Justin's steadfast personality and fun-loving character illuminated the garage that specific evening. There was no shortage of voice impressions or subtle jokes fired by him that night. As we all spontaneously and simultaneously huddled in a circle to converse—looking like we were rearing up to play an intense game of duck-duck-goose—Justin's high school friends and college pals quickly became acquainted with each other. War stories and precious memories were rehashed by each party as everyone boarded the bus whose only stop was memory lane. "Hey Justin, remember when" was the start of a plethora of sentences spoke that night. And that evening I also lost track of how many times I was referred to as "C-Willy" or "Little Wills."

    Justin, although not having seen his high school friends in months, picked up right where he left off with his old pals as if he was just with them the day before. And for his college friends who he had lived with only a couple weeks prior, the conversations continued effortlessly without the need to bridge any gap. As we sat in a circular form, there wasn't a rekindling of any flame with either Justin and his high school pals or college friends, because the fire was already blazing brightly—and certainly was never smothered from carelessness or extinguished by a rainfall. And as I recall, the official meeting of his *old* and *new* comrades went so well that some of them still stay in touch with each other from time to time. So rather than Justin being burdened with the decision of holding dear to him something old *or* something new, he was and is fortunate to possess both something old *and* something new—in relation to his current state of friendships. A great deal of this fact is accredited to Justin's transparent and authentic character. I've stated it once, I'll state it now, and I'm sure I will state it again, but with respect to my brother; what you see is what you get with Justin.

CAMERON JAMES WILLIAMS

Just Another Trophy on the Shelf

Justin's four years at Case Western Reserve University were the toughest and most arduous four years of his life up until that point—although he would never boastfully recognize it publicly. His level-headedness and confidence in himself allowed him to excel, yet again, in another classroom setting. Case Western is known for its exceptional engineering program. With that being said, he breezed by every obstacle with only a scar or two to show—and those were from the football field. His elevated mental acumen paired with an undying determination guided him to success in the classroom. He approached each step of college one at a time—methodically placing one foot in front of the other—and covered a journey extending for miles throughout his tenure at the school. The labor he sowed reaped a multitude of fruits, both tangible and intangible, other than that of receiving his diploma at the end of the fourth year.

In Justin's senior year, just before graduation, he was awarded an engineering award. This highly sought-after plaque—in which I forget the name—was one of the most prestigious and prominent honors allocated within the engineering field. The selective congratulation was granted to three engineering students—voted on by the cohort of the entire engineering personnel—

and was accompanied with a five-hundred-dollar cash prize for each student. The awardees were chosen on the basis of "exemplifying the essence of what it means to be an engineer throughout all four years at the university." There was no bias in the election process of the professors because frankly none of them had any skin in the game, so they made their decision solely on an objective foundation. My family and I happened to find out about Justin's award as we were having dinner a few weeks before his graduation. He casually mentioned that friends and family were invited to the award ceremony that the engineering department was hosting to present the plaques to him and two other students the day of graduation. Justin was enthused and humbled he was chosen by his engineering teachers but shrugged it off and completely underplayed the importance of the award. Out of the hundreds of engineering students who gravitated to Case Western from all corners of the world—some of the brightest minds on the planet—a young man who was raised two and a half hours away was unanimously viewed as one of the three most deserving pupils to be acknowledged for the illustrious engineering honor.

    On the day of Justin's graduation, after wrapping up his engineering ceremony, my family and I found our seats in preparation to watch all the soon-to-be graduates receive their diploma. We sat there for what felt like a millennium, patiently waiting for Justin's name to be announced over the loudspeaker (they proceeded in alphabetic order, so he was designated in the last bunch of students). Alas, "Justin Williams, summa cum laude" was spoken through the loudspeaker. My parents were more than prepared with their cameras ready to capture the perfect photo. Justin was extremely communicative with my family and me about everything except his accolades, so we were unaware that he was dubbed with the summa cum laude status. The Latin phrase "summa cum laude" quite literally means "with highest distinction." Justin's categorization was extremely fitting and the cherry on top to his decorative academic career.

Instead of viewing his graduation as the finish line and a time to turn complacent, Justin viewed it as the starting point for the remainder of his life. He recognized deep within him that he still had bigger fish to fry. Although tremendously content with where he was positioned at that point in time, Justin was never one to settle. He knew further self-imposed limits were to be pushed; adversity inevitably lied ahead ready for him to overcome; and unclaimed respect of an entire new set of individuals was patiently waiting to be claimed. Furthermore, Justin was alert of the fact that potential life was always waiting to be actualized and lived in the present moment—and his college graduation surely didn't alter that.

Broader horizons awaited him; as were tests to his self-confidence and positive mindset; and unquestionably an increasing number of transcendent portals were waiting to be found and more deeply entered—leading into enlightened dimensions within him that were not yet manifested. Justin spent the previous twenty-plus years of his life chiseling his desired image of his chosen character, and assuredly this masterpiece of a sculpture was not yet complete—although the artist was captivated by the ever-flowing beauty at that and every particular moment in time. In other words, Justin's saunter across the stage in his cap and gown at Case Western University was merely the end of a chapter—but the climax wasn't even reached yet in his eyes—and a new chapter and story was just beginning.

Conclusion to Part 1: Pre-Miranda

In sum, what have we learned thus far? Initially, we laid the groundwork for how *The 2650 Mile Aisle* appears at face value—which is a narrative that is a substitute for a best man speech. Additionally, the superficial motive of embarking on this written entertaining and romantic journey is to note how my brother, Justin, and soon-to-be sister-in-law, Miranda, are steering away from a conventional wedding—and instead embarking on their own journey of hiking the Pacific Crest Trail to officially pledge their vows. *The 2650 Mile Aisle*, in fact, highlights the above points, but it goes substantially deeper below the surface to provide an elevated meaning to the text.

In "Part 1: Pre-Miranda," after surfacing the housekeeping elements, we started to penetrate extensively below the surface to invoke the motivationally stimulating elements and effects of this writing. By describing in-depth through a multitude of different accounts and situations Justin was involved in throughout his life—in what would best be described as a cross between a biography and storytelling style—we learned a great deal of what makes Justin, effectually Justin. Through my eyes of these first-hand experiences and/or observations, the feelings of inspiration deep inside my being were formulated precisely into words to capture the full meaning of each occurrence. The intention was for the reader to embody these reciprocated feelings as he/she followed along. These similar emotions will be injected into "Part 2: Post-Miranda" as Miranda is introduced, although perhaps in a different light or angle.

But to recap, in Part 1, our complete introduction and description of Justin was spelled out clearly through four major portions: Chapter 1, "Respect is Earned; Not Given"; Chapter 2, "A Man as a Boy"; Chapter 3, "The Only Way is Through", and Chapter 4, "New Beginnings." Throughout "Respect is Earned; Not Given," the main focus was on Justin's unique ability to gracefully demand respect and honor from individuals of varying statuses, ages, backgrounds, etc. Although seemingly an innate attribute, there is a root and cause within Justin to this effect displayed by him. Additionally, Justin's steadfast character signifies him as a symbol of what it truly means to be an older brother. This symbol of Justin's noble character brightly shined through among his classmates also, as he once deferred against campaigning to run for class president against a close friend, after Justin weighed and calculated the risk to reward ratio of the scenario. During the pages of "A Man as a Boy," courage, faith, and pushing the limits of life were a few focal aspects containing the highest form of value to be extracted from the written words. We dove into the deep end as the waters of real-life expositions referring to pushing the self-imposed limits of the intellect, body, willpower, and life in general were treaded. As we removed our life preservers, we swam to the bottom and recognized how courage and faith are key components to ascending the infinite levels of life in the perpetual progression and evolution of our being. Whether Justin's mental acumen, physical strength, or discipline of self-control was thoroughly outlined, an inside look at the key components of pushing the limits of life were actively presented in real-time. "The Only Way is Through" centered in on the inevitable truth that everybody faces adversity in life. In our case, Justin's challenges were specifically emphasized. To overcome obstacles in life Justin proved that a positive mindset is absolutely critical. Furthermore, confidence in one's self breeds an increased sense of genuine positivity—and an optimistic outlook is crucial to ingraining in one's self the utmost confidence at all times. Justin illustrated—via diagnosis of diabetes in eighth grade or by battling acne as a teenager, to name only a couple instances—how imperative an unflappable nature is in trumping any form of adversity in the present moment. Whatever the opposition, as seen, Justin demonstrated and continues to demonstrate his sureness of one of the only things he can actively control in life; his reaction. Alas, in "New Beginnings," all the previous elements were mended together as Justin progressed onto college at Case Western Reserve

University. This portion of his life was a reset of sorts—as the respect he received prior was given a clean slate, enhanced limits were ready to be ascended, and newer, more difficult adversity waited ahead. Justin passed the tests with flying colors, walking away from the school unscathed with an engineering degree, engineering award, and a completely different group of tight-knit friends that would do anything for him.

So far, so good, right? But this picture is nowhere near being painted entirely—at least that's what Justin would attest. But before we close the chapter on Case Western and this portion of Part 1 entirely, one more essential item must be mentioned, which will be one of our starting points in Part 2. Take a wild guess at what this vital moment is. Anyone? You guessed it. It is the official meeting of Justin and Miranda at Case Western University at the end of their junior year. Hence, this glimpse into the pivotal moment will bring "Part 1: Pre-Miranda" to a closure. Superman and Wonder Woman will finally unite in "Part 2: Post-Miranda." Alone, each superhero is powerful, but together they are capable of moving mountains. I don't know about you, but my Spidey sense are tingling (wait that's the wrong comic).

Justin, on his own, possesses the esoteric capability of discovering (partially) analogous portals within himself to arrive at a liberating and rare place traveled by few—thus allowing him to surpass self-imposed limits with great courage and confidence—going above and beyond any element of conscious choice in his life. Justin's actions and examples mentioned are simply a signpost, or indicator, of truth that the access to courage, positivity, and freedom is, in fact, attainable. And surely if Justin has access, the power forever remains accessible within you and me as well. Although both Justin and Miranda face drudgery and misery in life at times—being seemingly locked in the chains of mental imprisonment inside of their heads, yet less frequently—Miranda has similarly found the source of where peace of mind and creative genius lives. In "Part 2: Post-Miranda," our quest will continue to unveil the source and origin of this mentioned portal, and through examples learn how that potential power is manifested. Alright, now time for a thirty-second TV timeout. See you soon!

PART 2: POST-MIRANDA

Part 2: Post-Miranda

Introduction

What is marriage? It seems as if it has become such a normal part of today's society. It's a word that gets breezed by when said or thrown around nonchalantly. The first technical definition of 'marriage' in Google's Oxford Dictionary search results is "the legally or formally recognized union of two people as partners in a personal relationship (historically and in some jurisdictions specifically a union between a man and a woman)."[1] This definition is not up for debate as any sane individual would agree that's what marriage means. Some people marry their high school sweetheart. Others marry their true love found in college. And many more marry someone they come across at the workplace or run into at a sporting event by pure fate. Whatever the reason—there is a reason why two individuals choose to marry each other. Some people simply want to start their own family. Others may have truly found their soulmate. And some people don't put much thought into the choice and drift where life takes them. The common statistic most people chuck around like a hot potato is that fifty percent of marriages end in a divorce. But in reality, that statistic isn't necessarily true, at least anymore. With that being said, as of 2018, the numbers aren't too far off their mark. Studies show approximately 42-45% of first marriages end in divorce, 60% of second marriages end in divorce, and 73% of third marriages end prematurely.[2] A 45% divorce rate is an indisputably staggering percentage for two individuals who promised to love each other for the rest of their lives.

    But why do so many marriages terminate ahead of time? This discussion is unquestionably a murky one with varying responses—for those who are currently married, have been married, and for those who have yet to be married. The effective reason I have concluded for the shocking statistic is that a vast majority of individuals carry out their surface-level marriage plans on account of the first dictionary definition of 'marriage,' when there is a second definition. The alternative dictionary definition of marriage is "a combination or mixture of two or more elements."[1] This definition holds a deeper, more meaningful interpretation of the word marriage as well as to the two partaking individuals involved in this type of relationship. Rather than being an activity, the second definition of marriage invokes a greater sense of living in togetherness.

THE 2650 MILE AISLE

I believe Justin and Miranda are slated towards the second definition of marriage. Now obviously the first definition will remain true for them additionally, as they are going to become official partners on paper. But their relationship and blended connection, or fusion, with each other is one that this first definition doesn't serve justice towards. Further, "a combination or mixture of two or more elements" is significantly more fitting for their situation. Justin and Miranda are unique creatures. They look like any other blond couple if you were to pass them on the street. They laugh. They smile. They'll hold the door for you. They agree with each other. They disagree with each other. But what differentiates them is the way they look at the world. Their vantage points of discernible first principles align with each other rather eerily. When both of them look at the world—and in themselves—they see a sphere of abundance and opportunities waiting to be seized. When both of them gaze into one of Mother Nature's expansive creations, they become one with it—and evidently one with her. As self-confident as Justin and Miranda are, when adventuring in nature, they surrender the image of themselves to join with something greater beyond their bodies. This capitulation of self and sense of oneness with the whole Universe is a major reason for choosing to initiate a 2650-mile journey to begin with. Both Justin and Miranda would agree that things few and far between surpass their love for hiking and being outdoors.

Justin and Miranda each love themselves more than they love anybody else on the planet. I say this with the most positive outlook because a high degree of this is healthy and absolutely necessary to progress in life. They are both intensely aware of the magnitude of endless love that exists in the Universe. Simply because they love themselves dearly, it doesn't deter or reduce the love they are able to impart to others. To be frank, I somewhat jokingly think Justin and Miranda would each marry themselves if they were allowed. But to be honest, they very well may have created this union of marriage within themselves—probably subconsciously—at some point in their lives. Proof of this is the wholeness and self-confidence each of them genuinely live with. They trust themselves to the highest degree because they are sure that's where the power of creation lies. I believe the above reasons are why Justin and Miranda are so incredibly magnetized towards each other. But contrary to magnets, like absolutely recognize like, and Justin and Miranda are two peas in the same pod. The characteristics and distinctions each of them distinguishes as sacred and savor in themselves is what they see in one another and what attracts them to each other. I have not entered into either Justin or Miranda's minds lately, but the heightened emotions that arise and feelings of submissiveness both of them feel when looking at the immeasurable size and beauty of a mountain range are the same exact feelings as when Justin and Miranda stare into each other's eyes.

When Justin and Miranda spend intimate time with each other, a liberating breath seems to wash over them. As confident and self-loving as both of them are, this all seems to subside when they are merged together. The confidence and love still remain—but in a different light—as both of them become vulnerable to the other party in pure bliss and positive intentions. Their internal power does not disappear; rather they pass their sacred power back and forth. This is the true definition of faith and progression; trusting in something that is unknown and can't be seen, yet knowing it exists and will propel you forward. Justin gives an ounce of his inner power to Miranda—opening up space for growth, yet at the moment becoming deficient—and in return, Miranda passes back a pound of her power, which then takes the place of the initial 'give.' As she gives her innate power, she also becomes vulnerable for the moment as Justin's power is replenished and enhanced. Justin then returns the power in a larger sum to renew her potency and then some. This process continues perpetually—give first, receive, give first, receive, etc.—the passing of powers back and forth. None of the above would be possible if both Justin and Miranda, although absolutely sure of themselves, don't initially become vulnerable to each other.

CAMERON JAMES WILLIAMS

What a beautiful sight it is to watch Justin and Miranda learn and grow together in their relationship, livelihoods, and life in general. But above is only one outlook on how to place words to the meaning of their personal relationship with each other. The true meaning of marriage may be stated in a slew of different ways, all with the same endpoint—just as every stream or river all ends up at the ocean.

Yet another perspective of stating the true meaning of marriage can be accredited to the birth of Napoleon Hill's 'life principles' (this guy interviewed 500 of the most successful people of his time; he knew what he was talking about). Although not as specified towards marriage—and perhaps more so of benefit to business tycoons or research study groups—Hill's following principle is certainly capable of orienting itself to and including marriage under its definition. Napoleon Hill's concept of the "Master Mind" group, in his famous book *Think and Grow Rich*,[3] is one of many ideas he contributes to guaranteed success in life. The "Master Mind" may be defined as "Coordination of knowledge and effort, in a spirit of harmony, between two or more people, for the attainment of a definite purpose."[4] Hill's mentioned "Master Mind" is capable of precisely relating to a handful of marriages. Justin and Miranda fit under this category. The reason they qualify as a "Master Mind" group is because their intentions and definitive purpose in life situate exactly in line. Justin and Miranda wake up every morning to push the limits of themselves and life itself. They are always seeking to learn, progress, and become the best versions of themselves—all while fully active in the present moment without worrying about the future or angry about the illusion of past. No matter what trivial things they may disagree upon in coming years, this first principle will forever be set in stone. The capabilities of growth and abundance are amplified exponentially when their potentialities are multiplied. Justin and Miranda—on their own as individuals—are extremely powerful and capable of creating a positive impact while serving their time on this earth. But together, they currently actualize this potential and will continue to be capable of achieving unfathomable things in life. Napoleon Hill mentions the economic and psychic features of the "Master Mind" group. The economic-related benefit is obviously an abundance of wealth, while the psychic aspect is slightly more abstract. "There are only two known elements in the whole Universe, energy and matter."[5] Hill goes on to state, "No two minds ever come together without, thereby, creating a third, invisible, intangible force which may be likened to a third mind."[6] Furthering his point, Hill definitively proclaims, "It is a well-known fact that a group of electric batteries will provide more energy than a single battery…The brain functions in a similar fashion."[7] I'm not sure if Justin or

Miranda have ever even read Napoleon Hill's book, but certainly they know what he is referring to when he discussed the "Master Mind" group. Individually, they may be able to push a mound of dirt, or maybe even a hill (pun intended). But together, Justin and Miranda move mountains.

CHAPTER 6: A MATCH MADE IN (WHATEVER YOUR BELIEF SYSTEM)

So we started Part 2 somewhat backwards, beginning at the culminating point—marriage. Before we discuss Justin and Miranda's fusion further, answers to the following questions must be provided: Who is Miranda? How did Justin and Miranda meet? What makes them a perfect match? How do Justin and Miranda enhance each other's already solidified foundation of adventure, and character in general? These above questions, among numerous other telling inquiries and narratives of Justin and Miranda's fusion, will be responded to and thoroughly explored throughout the remainder of *The 2650 Mile Aisle*.

CAMERON JAMES WILLIAMS

Welcome to the Party, Miranda

Who is Miranda Huiting? Differing from Justin, who I have known my entire life, I have only known Miranda for four to five years. But it honestly feels like a lifetime. At the surface, she is a normal blond girl who grew up in the beautiful scenery of Colorado. There she lived a normal life and was raised by a normal family—having a mom, dad, one brother, and one sister. At first glance, Miranda is normal. But extensively permeate beyond her flesh inward and it will be found that Miranda is far from normal, or ordinary. Frankly stated, this woman is extraordinary. How would I describe Miranda? Disarmingly intelligent, independent to the nth degree, yet exceedingly humble, all while immovably self-confident. The adjectives in the previous sentence are only a few of the vast field of words that attempt to describe her character.

With that being said, words have trouble precisely unfolding Miranda's being due to her intensely rich character. It is like trying to explain the feelings felt when eating your favorite food, watching your favorite movie, drinking a fine wine, or for some people—like Miranda—the feeling of being in the wilderness. Words simply do not serve the experience justice in these instances, among many other blissful scenarios. To truly understand how a slice of pizza tastes, one must eat

THE 2650 MILE AISLE

a slice of pizza. Similarly, to truly understand who Miranda is and the precious intricacies she embodies, one must spend a day with her. Obviously, that is not possible, so I will relay these feelings through real-life narratives and by placing fitting symbols (words) in their proper spots to invoke an exact replica of sentiment—as if the reader was granted the privilege of meeting Miranda.

Miranda was always a champion in the classroom, and nothing changed in her college years at Case Western Reserve University. In high school, she finished her career near the top percentile of her fellow students. Knowledge was always absorbed and acquired rather easily by Miranda. Additional to her intrinsic brilliance, her persistent efforts in and out of the classroom thrusted her to unparalleled heights, being viewed as the cream of the metaphoric crop in her school. Miranda is the type of person that when she sets her mind to do or achieve something, she is going to do it. I guarantee that Miranda was consciously aware she would be a leading rank in her class before she even entered high school. Any obstacle in her way was trampled as she kept a pure heart and clear eyes set on the prize. Before the gun was fired to start the analogous race, she had already crossed the finish line and was standing on the podium in her mind. Whether this definitiveness is a natural or learned trait I do not know. Whatever the case, the determination and sureness of herself is evidently forged into her character today. "Mind over matter" is an age-old saying, but Miranda truly realizes the meaning of these three nonchalantly thrown around words. Straightforwardly, Miranda knows what she can control in her life, and one of these elements apparent to her is being in control of her destiny.

Somewhat ironic to what is expected from someone with such a high degree of self-assuredness, Miranda comprehensively enjoys visiting Mother Nature—who is unpredictable and can never be understood or known entirely. The thing she is least sure of, the wilderness, is one of the places she gravitates towards most. I believe it is at the temple of Mother Nature where Miranda becomes comfortably impuissant to such an incomprehensible, powerful place. It is there where she is not capable of complete knowledge, but that is okay, and she is well aware of that. The immeasurability of Mother Nature and the Universe invokes a sense of awe and wonder to all those who submit to them. This awe leads to liberating feelings that remove the heaviest of burdens off of anyone's shoulders. In Miranda's case, it opens her mind—even for split-second increments—to fathom the unfathomable. When adventuring nature, Miranda's sturdy sense of self dissipates as she surrenders to the grander being that she becomes one with. Anyone who has looked up into the stars or into a mountain range—with a thoughtless clear mind and even clearer heart—can attest to the connection felt with Mother Nature especially in those moments.

For Miranda, these emotions via the wilderness were imbued frequently into her, as adventure was right out the backdoor of her Colorado home growing up. Only yards from Miranda's back porch were miles of vast plains crawling with wildlife. From prairie dogs to coyotes, to the most beautiful butterflies the eye has ever seen, these critters among many other of their friends in the neighborhood could be seen in a day spent on the Colorado plains. With no shortage of passion, Miranda would explore this terrain exhaustively for hours on end as this immense swath of land was adjacent to a colossal mountain range, which were always capped with glistening white snow regardless of the season—as if it were a painting. After graduating from the exploration of the great plains (not the notorious Great Plains but still pretty great) in her younger years, she continued her everlasting pursuit of Mother Nature as she grew older by hiking the plentiful miles upon miles of mountain ranges in Colorado (the Rocky Mountains...ever hear of them?). As many people may be frightened by the grandness of the mountains and their sweeping trails, that is exactly what excited Miranda and drew her towards them. By the time she reached high school, she was practically a hiking expert—as it was virtually in her blood by that point. But simply hiking five to ten-mile trails with forty-five-degree inclines and declines began to not challenge her anymore. Instead of settling and becoming complacent, she continued to hike lengthier and more difficult trails, always content with the trail under her feet, yet still alert that further limits to be pushed awaited her.

Just as Miranda was certain of her abilities in the classroom, she was determined to achieve anything she set her mind to in Mother Nature's classroom as well. Miranda's brilliance in school and on trails are merely two particular instances where she allocates the potent power that exists within her. Throughout Part 2, we will examine further areas of greatness where Miranda unleashes her immovable characteristics. One thing I've learned is certain with Miranda: any task she undertakes she will proceed wholeheartedly. Muhammad Ali, one of the greatest boxers of all time, has a similar winning personality. He once expressed this truth when he said, "It's a lack of faith that makes people afraid of meeting challenges, and I always believed in myself."[1] Ali must have meant exactly what he stated because similarly at a different time he also announced, "He who is not courageous enough to take risks will accomplish nothing in life."[2] Miranda, not the most diehard of sports fans, may not be all too familiar with Muhammad Ali's decorated boxing history, but she can absolutely relate to what he said in these two quotes. And Muhammad Ali is unaware of Miranda's notable history, but these words might as well have been describing her. In any case, I know two things are true regarding Muhammad Ali and Miranda Huiting: Miranda is too smart to enter a ring with Ali; and Muhammad Ali is smart enough to not enter a classroom or an outdoor exploratory competition (I think that's a real thing) with Miranda.

CAMERON JAMES WILLIAMS

Miranda, Meet Justin; Justin, Meet Miranda

Once upon a time, there was knight in shining armor at Case Western University who would write anonymous weekly letters to the woman of his dreams. Every week the princess—to her despair—would peruse the campus diligently for her charming secret admirer. She would travel from east to west, and north to south, in search for the man of her dreams, but every week would return to her dormitory emptyhanded. Roses were sent bi-weekly with a clue of the location and identity of this masked man. The letters he wrote were comparable to the passionate scripts of a historic poet—with emotions poured onto the endless pages, filled to the brim with romance and tenderness—certain to melt the princess's heart. One week at the beginning of her junior year at the school, the princess solved the puzzle, found the man of her dreams, and they galloped off into the sunset via a horse and chariot. The rest was history.

This is not the story of how Miranda and Justin met and started an intimate relationship. In fact, the specific occurrence was rather anticlimactic—and normal—which was surprising considering Justin and Miranda were involved. Anyways, Justin and Miranda were introduced to each other by a mutual friend. The only true part of the above mythical tale is that the initial

THE 2650 MILE AISLE

congregation of Justin and Miranda was, in fact, at the beginning of their junior years at Case Western (Maybe it was the end of their sophomore year. I have an unreliable memory; back off... jeez.) Regardless, since Miranda was studying for her nutrition degree to become a dietitian, and Justin was pursuing his engineering career, their paths never crossed until that inceptive soirée in the middle of their college tenure.

If I remember correctly from the peanut gallery and through the grapevine, they actually didn't even hit it off the first few times they were together. They mutually, gradually opened up to one another and then after that, the rest was history. Presumptively speaking, I believe this delayed attraction was due to both of their escalated self-love and independent personalities. One may conclude that both of them thought the other was "too good to be true" as Justin saw his reflection in Miranda, and vice versa. Perhaps even their expansive minds were unable to come to the conclusion that there was someone on the planet that reciprocated his and her characteristics—generally speaking—nearly exactly. Or maybe both of them were uneasy of the commitment to another human being, devoting themselves to one another in a relationship, consequently opening up their hearts unconditionally. Whatever the case, all the uncertainty faded away with time as their analogous walls were climbed over or dug under. After a few weeks, in typical Justin and Miranda fashion, they both simultaneously aimed to navigate to the other side of the other's wall as they learned the type of person each of them was. And you bet your bottom dollar that if Justin and Miranda consciously chose to embark on the journey to *win* the other's heart, the process was well-thought-out and methodically planned from start to finish—certain of the end result.

    As similar as they were and are, both Justin and Miranda's nuances complement the other's character exceptionally. Their first principles of living replicate each other, but the way they arrive differs from time to time. Reflecting on their past from the present day, this is what enables them to truly enhance each other's lives and allows them to learn and grow together. Their relationship is indubitably one of give and take. For instance, due to their varying backgrounds, Miranda was and still is able to shed light to Justin on the vastness of Mother Nature—especially when considering the mountains in Pennsylvania compared to Colorado. In return, Justin's wittiness adds an extra dose of unexpectedness and flare to anyone's life—Miranda's included. With that being said, nobody keeps score of the exchange of benefits so to speak. Rather than being a transactional relationship or one based on utility, their independent natures warrant them to enjoy each other's company for the sake of the other's company; nothing more, nothing less.

Well-respected philosophers since time immemorial, from Socrates to Immanuel Kant, among an array of others, have dissected the flaws of living "a means to and end" type of lifestyle. For instance, contemporary spiritual teacher and best-selling author, Eckhart Tolle, discusses the transcendence above a "means to an end" mentality in his book, *A New Earth: Awakening to Your Life's Purpose* in the chapter, "Your Inner Purpose":

The negation of time in what you do also provides the link between your inner and outer purposes, between Being and doing. When you negate time, you negate the ego. Whatever you do, you will be doing extraordinarily well, because the doing itself becomes the focal point of your attention. Your doing then becomes a channel through which consciousness enters this world. This means there is quality in what you do, even in the most simple action, like turning the pages in the phone book or walking across the room. The main purpose for turning the pages is to turn the pages; the secondary purpose is to find a phone number. The main purpose for walking across the room is to walk across the room; the secondary purpose is to pick up a book at the other end, and the moment you pick up the book, that becomes your main purpose.[1]

Instead of acting as each other's missing piece of the puzzle, both Justin and Miranda are whole and complete in their own perspectives as is.

While challenging each other and expediting one another's growth in life, Justin and Miranda have remained independent—yet together—throughout their relationship. Perhaps a better, yet paradoxical or oxymoronic way of stating this is that Justin and Miranda were and continue to be independently united.

Here we are in 2020, and still nothing has changed between them since 2013-2014. Their relationship continues to remain fresh and lively, as if it was their senior year at Case Western. Truthfully, their connection becomes noticeably closer and further engrained every time I see them together. Justin and Miranda cannot get enough of each other, and I don't mean that in a sexual way, as their fusion to one another is increasingly more meaningful with longer-lasting substance. Their attraction penetrates way beyond skin and flesh, as their hearts and souls are united as one.

So although not the tale of a knight in shining armor and princess as we originally expected, the meeting of two minds is always a beautiful happening to observe and experience. But before we discuss Prince Charming and Cinderella's trot into the sunset on their horse and buggy (or begin their 2650-mile hike of the Pacific Crest Trail), we must first explore what genuinely makes Justin and Miranda a perfect match and how they ignited an entire new flame of adventure in one another that was not previously fathomed, from the time period of their college years up until

THE 2650 MILE AISLE

today. Now, at once—Miranda, meet Justin; and Justin, meet Miranda. If only both of you knew where this adventure of life would take you two young lovers.

Winter Break: Plus One Edition

I remember the first time my family and I met Miranda like it was yesterday. It was the winter vacation of Justin and Miranda's junior year at Case Western. As I'm sure you all know, winter vacation in college is no short stint—lasting roughly a month, give or take a few days. So when they (whoever *they* are) say vacation, they literally use the word to its highest order. I can't speak for my family's inner feelings as much as my own, but I recall having mixed emotions of the month-long visit from someone who was a complete stranger to me at the time. According to my recollection, I viewed it as a bitter-sweet welcoming. Most of the bitterness was the childish, immature part of myself bidding for the reigns, delusional of the supposition that somebody was trying to take my older brother away from me. That mindset was like a selfish child with the "mine" and "me, me, me" mentality. It was akin to a kindergartener who brought an entire package of cookies to school that mommy purchased yet refusing to spare even a single treat to any of his classmates. The metaphoric sweet side of me—the half that was grown-up and recognized by myself and others as more desirable—was eager to meet the person my brother's heart had fallen for. This mature, higher-energy portion was also happy to see my brother happy for his own sake, regardless of the attempted diversion from my lower-energy side of greedy tendencies. Realistically, no matter what my state of mind was—immature or mature—Miranda was visiting regardless.

Immediately upon Justin and Miranda's entrance through the front door, any iota of doubt I was previously battling dissipated into the atmosphere. Miranda skipped the traditionally expected inauthentic and generic "What's going on?" and "I like your shoes" and talked to my family and myself as if she had known us for years. As she bypassed the robotic meaningless small talk, she showed she was a human being, without a speck of pretentiousness in sight. Miranda treated us like we were human beings. We all hit it off and chatted about a range of different topics—both superficial and more intellectually demanding subjects—as she became acquainted with her place of stay for the next thirty days. Exaggeratedly speaking, although I hadn't seen my brother in over a month, Miranda claimed my undivided attention as I was impressed with respect to the type of character she was. Miranda was straightforward, yet easy-going; genuine, yet an open-minded free thinker. It didn't take long to realize how her words were packed with substance and weren't wasted. Miranda's quality over quantity approach to speaking, and life, was apparent and absolutely appreciated. Simply put, she didn't talk just to hear herself speak. For continuous moments at separate parts of our earliest conversations, I was convinced I was talking to a female version of Justin. A slight portion of me debated if Justin invented a way to clone himself in one of his engineering classes in college. As I attempted to rip her wig off when she wasn't looking—to my pleasant surprise, it was officially confirmed—she was the real Miranda Huiting. And my brother—who escaped my silent accusation of him being an evil scientist—was the same old, lovable Justin.

One thing strikingly evident I noticed instantly was Justin and Miranda's sense of togetherness. From the most trivial of activities of say, doing the laundry, to more serious situations, such as playing a board game on the same team as each other (Hey, on winter break, board games are a pretty damn big deal), they reminded me of Cheech and Chong (ironically, although a Colorado-native, Miranda was not an avid marijuana smoker; nor was Justin). Or peanut butter and jelly. Or beer and a belly. Or a Port-a-Potty that is smelly. I think you get the point. Whatever the analogy of choice is, simply stated, they went together hand and hand. I'm not kidding, literally any activity they partook in was executed in perfect harmony. Whether they were cooking, making adult beverages, adventuring outdoors, or even watching television—Miranda was the coffee to Justin's donut (alright fine, I'll stop now).

As we already know that in any activity Justin and Miranda engage, it can be assured that they will approach said activity full-tilt, harnessing all their energy towards the task. Cooking meals over winter break was no exception to their unwavering principle. Amazingly enough, watching them cook the lasagna they prepared the one evening was like observing rocket scientists from NASA assemble a spacecraft prior to launching a mission to Mars. Both Miranda and Justin were the head-chefs and assistants simultaneously—keeping the end goal in mind—a delicious Italian meal. One of them stirred while the other measured, and then practically telepathically—without any words or motions exchanged—they swapped roles without skipping a beat. The accuracy in the timing of combining all the ingredients together was also beautifully executed (it was calculated down to the second). I thought I knew what efficiency was before their culinary performance, but after witnessing Justin and Miranda's coherence in the kitchen, they opened my eyes to a completely different level of productivity. To this day I can still reminisce and taste the perfectly tender ground meat, the ideal texture of layered noodles, and the exactly right amount of chunky tomato sauce. Needless to say, accents of the love and energy infused into the exquisite lasagna dish treated my palate politely as well. (Chef Boyard-who?)

Alright, so Justin and Miranda can make a tasty dinner; what's the big deal? This type of uniformity and connectedness also spilled over into every single other one of their undertakings; for example, when they were going to explore Mother Nature the one afternoon. The rough sketch of their day's itinerary was to go for a hike and fire a rifle a few times at the shooting range. Once again, without an apparent announced divide-and-conquer plan, Justin and Miranda spontaneously split up to prepare for their day in the wilderness. Cheech (Justin) gathered the gun, ammunition, and two spare jackets in case the temperature dropped. And Chong (Miranda) stayed inside and arranged a cooler, packed two lunches, and gathered other miscellaneous hiking necessities for the day ahead. At the moment I heard Justin close the garage door behind him, Miranda was spreading the last swipe of mayonnaise on the second sandwich, as the hiking equipment and cooler were already placed in the backseat of my brother's car. That winter vacation was a 'first' for both Miranda and Justin. Miranda shot a gun for the first time in her life, courtesy of Justin's precise guidance. And Justin learned for the first time how to clean up after himself in the kitchen after cooking a meal, with Miranda's mentoring of course (C'mon, Justin, you didn't expect me to take it too easy on you, did you?).

Upon completion of their eventful day with Mother Nature, unplugging from quote end quote

THE 2650 MILE AISLE

normal society, it was only fitting a mixed adult beverage followed to set a cherry on top of their blissful day. As I witnessed a few days earlier with the lasagna, the invisible lab coats and goggles were positioned onto Professor Miranda and Professor Justin's bodies and faces after they unpacked the hiking supplies. Their next creative alchemistic science experiment would be concocting exact ratios of one part alcohol and the remaining volume with a non-alcoholic drink of choice—completed with a garnish of course. Now when I say the ratios of their mixed beverages were exact, I mean they were exact; there was not a drop more or a drop less of the chosen recipe. Once again, the bartending duties of measuring and shaking were performed interchangeably. The transition was so smooth and fluent, it was as if I was attending an opera enacted on Broadway. Although their actions behind the makeshift bar were smooth, the beverages were even smoother. Believe it or not, they were crafted so well that I think my dad unconsciously left a tip on the table, forgetting we were in the dining room and not at a bar in downtown Pittsburgh before a Steelers playoff game.

    It was obvious that winter vacation many years ago that Miranda was as efficient with her time as Justin was—if not more so. Even when they were lounging around in the morning before starting their action-packed days, they gulped some coffee down while simultaneously cooking a five-star breakfast to fuel up for the day ahead. After Justin cleaned up the dishes (thank you, Miranda), instead of both of them unconsciously looking out the window with a thousand-yard stare, they definitively knew what they wanted to achieve that specific day. Even if they weren't immersing in a physically strenuous pursuit, such as hiking, they still used their time constructively whatever the case may have been. For example, during the most conventionally mindless activity — watching television — Justin and Miranda discovered a way to wring the highest degree of benefit from their chosen program. I forget if they were watching the Discovery Channel or the History Channel, but I recall the thought-provoking discussion that followed suit at the commercials. They were dissecting every element of the show from every possible angle to gain the deepest understanding that was attainable. Their intelligent conversation, agreeing to disagree at times, was like they were in the court of law. Their discussion of the show was like they were, at once, both the judge and jury in the same courtroom — interpreting all sides of the case — attempting to objectively comprehend the topic of dialogue from an unbiased perspective. Instead of losing brain cells at a rapid pace from viewing a reality TV show, they gained some sort of benefit while sitting in front a big screen that had loads of images and sounds coming from it. I'm not sure if this was the case or not, but if Miranda had in fact clicked the remote to turn on the Discovery or History Channel, I would have known she was 'the one' right then and there—only a week after our initial meeting.

Yes, Justin and Miranda's intelligence is impressive; and so are their positive mindsets, unquestionably. But arguably what's potentially more astonishing than their smarts, positivity, or togetherness amongst each other—is their togetherness and balance within each of themselves. In the purest sense of togetherness, or companionship, neither Justin nor Miranda perceive themselves as lacking anything and view themselves as whole on their own—without the need to supplement a void with the temporary fill of somebody else. A somewhat different perspective of saying this same point is that both Justin and Miranda, whether learned or innate is beside the point (I personally think it's a mix of both), are able to find the mean between any extreme.

They remind me of the famous philosopher, Aristotle, and his basic principle of the "Golden Mean." He laid this enlightened notion down over 2500 years ago, but it still proves true today. Time and time again the meaning is described sharply throughout countless traditions and philosophies, although using different words. But Aristotle's "Golden Mean" states that, "Moral behavior is the mean between two extremes—at one end excess, the other deficiency. Find the position between those two extremes, and you will be acting morally."[1] And this is exactly how Justin and Miranda strive to live each of their lives, and they squarely execute continuously. Somehow, Justin and Miranda have discovered the perfect balance between surrendering and being disciplined; between patience and persistence; between carelessness and carefulness; between consciously thinking and emotionally feeling; between forever arriving yet never ceasing to explore; and between stillness and progression—while alertly straddling the fence connecting the controllable and uncontrollable factors of life.

    Ultimately this exact mean between the two extremes can be considered a 'flow state.' The flow state of living is like the water of a stream traversing down a hillside; its destination is determined yet it swirls where the current takes it. This flow is a state of mind and a way of life for both Justin and Miranda. And like a large oak tree in a treacherous rain and windstorm, they will bend but they will never break—as the trunk, roots, and foundation are extraordinarily embedded into the ground suffusing deep below the surface. That winter vacation would not be the last time I saw Miranda. And needless to say, nor would it be the last time Justin checked the 'plus one' box when returning home either.

No Rocky Meeting

A few summers ago, my family and I planned to visit Colorado as we had never been there. We were excited to experience the Rocky Mountains, Garden of the Gods, and the unique town of Boulder, among a list of other jaw-dropping vistas. As we were searching for an Airbnb or hotel to accommodate all of us, Justin reached out and said that Miranda's family offered to host us in their house for the week. We kindly accepted their invitation of generosity, as we were eager to finally meet them.

When my family and I arrived in Colorado, we buckled our seatbelts in the rental car and headed for the Huiting residence—not with an inkling of what to expect. They could have been the nicest of nice or the meanest of mean, and anything in between. The GPS declared our arrival, and everyone gathered themselves in the driveway to prepare to meet the family we would be living with for the next week. As we approached the door, the fresh scent of Colorado trees and flowers distracted our attention away from anything but the pleasant aroma. Without further distraction, we poked the doorbell. "Ding ding doo dah." And as the chime started fading away, the barrier swung open and there stood the Huiting family. Mrs. Huiting, Mr. Huiting, Miranda's younger sister, Larissa, and their older brother, Gannon, greeted us with hugs and hors d'oeuvres and made us feel at home immediately. Our sleeping quarters—which were caringly and thoughtfully assembled—were shown to us as the Huitings gave us some time to settle in. After a few minutes, Mrs. Huiting hollered down the stairs that dinner was going to be ready soon. I remember that I couldn't quite pin down which type of food was cooking, but I knew it smelled delicious. The Huiting family hospitality was top-notch from start to finish during our trip. Home-cooked dinners became the norm as the sun began to set behind the mountains, as well as breakfast when the sun peeped out from the same mountain range the following day—although a different view. Our family told them that we were not expecting any of the kind gestures they were firing our way and that we were more than grateful that they were simply hosting us—but they continued to feed and pamper us anyways.

The Williams family and Huiting family meshed instantly. By the second day, it already felt like we knew each other for a couple of years. It was a beautiful thing to be a part of two separate families, cultures, lifestyles—merging into one. Our families played board games, listened to music, and feasted together—like they were an extended family of ours and we were an extended family at theirs. Their cordiality was so splendid that I almost forgot we were actually visiting a family that we had never spoke to until a few days prior. They were exceptional hosts, and we were as good of guests. They added value to our lives, and we added value to theirs—how any proper relationship should transpire. My family and I arrived in Colorado with a long laundry list of activities we wanted to accomplish during our time near the Mile High City. The Huiting family was not only enthused to assist us in completing our itinerary activities, but they also gave suggestions on additional ventures that we may be interested in while we were there—that only locals had insight too.

    One of these inclusions into our itinerary was hiking in Rocky Mountain National Park. We already planned to hike our fair share, so this was a cherry on top to the mountainous adventures. Mr. Huiting joined us on our exploration that day—as Mrs. Huiting, Larissa, and Gannon held down the fort. The Huitings possessed more knowledge about the Rocky Mountains—and Colorado in general— than imaginable, and they weren't shy to share it. This certainly enhanced the experience by having a deeper understanding of where we were at or what we were doing. In other words, the Huitings were tour guides on steroids. As we approached the entrance gate to the trailhead of the Rocky Mountain National Forest, we were enlightened on its history, different trees and animals in the region, as well as other useful facts and information. And similar to Miranda, I noticed everyone else in the Huiting family carefully chose their words too, and they loaded them with substance. The car ride was over two hours long, but it absolutely didn't feel like it. Engaged conversations, the positive energy flowing in the vehicle, and obviously a healthy dosage of laughter made the travel a breeze—and unquestionably enjoyable. Gazing out of the car window at the immeasurable mountain range as the sun glistened off the snow-capped peaks and warmed our faces also aided in our delightful ride.

After traveling on a road that was also a cliff of the Rocky Mountains—looking down frightened to see our unfortunate fate below or ecstatic to embrace the slew of lush trees and wildlife underneath us—we arrived at the entrance of the Rocky Mountain National Forest. Or at least that's what we thought. After pacing around the locked gate to confirm that our eyes weren't deceiving us—and brainstorming ideas as to why the entrance was closed—we accepted the fact that our only option was to find another way into the park. We hopped back in the vehicle and traveled forty-five minutes to a different gate. Frankly, we could have driven around all day and everyone would have been just as content—since the views were astonishing, and the company in the car was just as precious. Our joyous spirits continued to overflow out of the windows across the mountain range as we approached the second gate. We parked and ended up having an absolutely incredible hike in the Rocky Mountain National Forest, but the car ride was just as incredible. That day definitively

THE 2650 MILE AISLE

established that *they* are right when *they* say that the journey is just as important as the destination.

After our exhaustive and rejuvenating day in the Rocky Mountains, we returned to the Huitings' house and enjoyed a meal courtesy of Mrs. Huiting that was just as satisfying as the hike, the car ride, and the quest to Colorado in its entirety. Our trip to Colorado was one I will never forget, as the Williams family and Huiting family joined together in unison—as there was certainly no rocky meeting.

CAMERON JAMES WILLIAMS

<u>Acquired Taste</u>

The "Acquired Taste" section of *The 2650 Mile Aisle* is arguably one of the most important parts of this piece of literature, as the particular instance described sums up who Justin is today. Although the contents of the chapter are extracted from a thirty-minute conversation Justin and I had while camping last year, the impact will last a lifetime. Justin's verbal expressions and determined truths embodied throughout our conversation are a microcosm of Justin's sincere character. To paint the picture and set the scene, Justin and I were sitting by the campfire—crafted by him, obviously—while our immediate family and Miranda were elsewhere enjoying other activities in the woods, or simply relaxing on a hammock. There was not a cloud in the gloaming sky as we were granted the privilege of clearly seeing every star up above our heads, from the North Star to the Big and Little Dipper. As if the silence of the night wasn't beautiful enough, with the crackling and popping of the campfire every so often, Justin and I started to discuss what an acquired taste truly was and what it meant.

Justin prefers pretty much everything in his life in its simplest form, from his selection of wardrobe to even the most complex of topics, such as engineering or the Universe. To reemphasize one of Albert Einstein's timeless quotes is, "If you can't explain it to a six-year-old, you don't understand it yourself."[1] Justin absolutely follows this KISS principle of "Keep it simple stupid,"[2] which is another way of stating Einstein's declaration. This simplistic, minimalistic attitude carries over into Justin's choice of beverages as well. Although a majority of the fluid that enters his body is water, he will indulge in coffee, wine, and beer. With that being said, this is where the acquired taste comes into play. He prefers his coffee black, his wine dry, and his beer hoppy — preferring an IPA over any other type of ale.

As we embraced the warmth of the campfire, I—having previously wrestled with solving the riddle of what an acquired taste was— surfaced the topic, curious of Justin's opinion on the matter. Personally speaking, years ago I used to drown my coffee in cream and sugar; now I drink it black. Also, when I first began indulging in alcohol, I would much rather sip a sweet, sugary wine over a dry wine; and now I reach for the dry wine on the shelf instead. I stated this to Justin and continued my partially unresolved statement of thought, tumultuous of the matter of the fact that sugar and cream was more palatable and *tastier* in one sense—yet I enjoyed black coffee to a higher degree. And these were my exact thoughts on the sweet wine to dry wine transition also. In an unfulfilling, childish, and animalistic light—before maturing—sweet wine *tastes* better, but the experience in its entirety of sipping on a dry wine blows the sweet wine out of the water.

I previously grappled to and fro, and back and forth, attempting to put words of how I felt on the acquired taste dilemma and eager to unveil the truth of the matter—with a definitive and concise conclusion. Obviously, physiologically a human being's palate matures and changes with age, but I knew that was only the surface-level understanding of the matter, and that there was a much deeper significance. Justin turned out to be my lifeline in this situation as I 'phoned a friend,' except I was not seeking to become a millionaire (shoutout to Regis Philbin). Instead, I was seeking something more enduring: truth and meaning. As the external sky was crystal clear that night, Justin helped to uncloud my mind in that thirty-minute discussion—providing clarity and peace of mind with his carefully picked words and thoughts.

At the end of our conversation, the camping trip was already well worth the trip, even though it was the first or second night. That evening, I was awarded the assist and Justin scored the goal, as he indisputably was the reason this metaphoric puck or ball crossed the goal line. His perspective was one of grace, of purity, and virtue. The following italicized paragraphs are a summary of what Justin and I concluded as to the meaning of what an acquired taste truly was and is:

THE 2650 MILE AISLE

An acquired taste occurs when the invisible, intangible essence, or pureness (spirit) of an outward thing or event resonates with the spirit and purity within a human being—which is also intangible. The physical form of the former only reaches, touches, and connects with the physical form of the tangible human body. But surely—we as human beings—are more than merely skin, bones, and organs. The life force beyond the human body that permeates inward of the said human form is the truth and a portion of the ultimate cause of life. Life is full of cause and effects—and the effects are simply a manifestation of the unseen, unmanifested inward cause. For example, an enormous skyscraper in New York City, beautifully architected and precise down to one sixty-fourth of an inch, was initially a thought in somebody's mind. The thought came from an indescribable, intangible place, yet was the cause of a massive, tangible structure that stands sturdy for decades.

Things without additives or excessiveness that are completely and utterly natural—speak not to the body of a human being—but to the soul and life force living within the body. Contrarily, if things—such as coffee or wine—contain additives or so-called enhancements (like sweeteners), the true essences are clouded as the desirous and lower-energy craving body seeks and finds the temporary, surface-level fulfillment. The soul and sacred power within the shell of the human body must be prevalent, present, and shining brightly to be receptive of these former—simple, natural, and genuinely fulfilling—things. For example, regarding the dry wine and black coffee, the experience exceeds just the tastes buds as a more complete appreciation of the beverage is perceived and embraced. Every single accent and layer of flavor is appreciated and enjoyed for what they are—with penetrative depth—without the false sense of need for artificial or superficial additives or deceitful enhancements. If the power and higher-energy life force within is not consciously active, the physical body (tastes buds included) take over unconsciously and continuously search and crave superficial, temporary forms instead—never exactly filling the empty void.

Extending further, the beauty of Mother Nature remains within her internally and intangibly, as does this same unseen force remain within the human body. For example, when we as human beings observe a flower, we—in our unconscious state—look at the external, end effect of the flower. What we don't recognize or see until we are in a conscious state of mind—letting our soul shine through our beings—is the internal life force and cause of the flower manifesting its glorious, external form. What is then seen is a living being that unknowingly overcame adversity and continued to persist, serving its exact purpose perfectly (being a flower) in its utmost natural state—nothing more and nothing less—in perfect timing and harmony. In this latter conscious state, there is a sense of oneness with the flower and life itself.

An acquired taste is present when the human body's transcendent life, spirit, or being is in the analogous driver's seat (rather than sitting in the passenger's seat) and links in communion to the purest state (spirit or life force) of any other being. Generally speaking—exceeding solely beverages—an acquired taste is when the true and natural essence within a human being is connected with the true and natural life force elsewhere alive in another shelled being. These pure, unspoiled, and divine 'things' within both said beings—although unseen—are the ultimate cause of life in general, and evidently specifically too. Like recognize like. The purity within each human being links to—like a key and a lock— the pure substances from our outer worlds. The external purity we perceive is only possible when our inner state of being matches that purity. And when so, the external beauty is potent and capable of stimulating the heightened mental, inner force, and elevated state of the human being. If in a lower, immature, animalistic, and temporary fulfillable state, the external forms will reflect precisely the lacking inner state. Only when the receptive mind, spirit, and soul are in a similar state of beauty, grace, virtue, and purity is when the external mirror reflects the same type of being—which is the actualized potential of life in its truest, most natural, harmonious and beautiful manifestation.

So what is an acquired taste? It boils down to the wholesome essence of experience. Until one has achieved and experienced this state, it is difficult to comprehend. Words are precious symbols, but no combination of the hieroglyphs serves justice to the deeper meaning of an acquired taste. Regarding wine, coffee, and beer, an acquired taste is enjoying and appreciating the experience exactly for what it is in the specific present moment; not craving more, lacking control, or wishing it any other way—but simply cherishing every sip as sacred. Less is more holds its structural integrity here. Yes, the dry wine is still intoxicating, but that's not the sole purpose of indulging in the beverage for Justin and Miranda. Each and every part of the process and experience is appreciated equally. The wine is not used strictly as a vehicle, or means, to become drunk. Instead, the dry wine is enjoyed for itself. From purchase to pour, every element of their experience is respected and relished as is.

    An acquired taste between two people is displayed more times than not by Justin and Miranda, as their purest and highest senses of being are aligned exactly, like the ancient Egyptian astronomers precisely aligned the pyramids in a north-south direction.[3] With that being said, possessing an acquired taste traverses beyond the particular forms of beverages and people—as it is a mindset and way of life in general. Although every moment in life is a battle to maintain an acquired taste vantage point, sometimes the pointless cravings of metaphoric cream and sugar prevail. The goal is to drink this analogous black coffee or dry wine for every moment of eternity. An acquired taste in its highest degree and most proper and truest form doesn't come and go but lasts forever. Justin and Miranda, who exercise the unique ability to access this inner portal more frequently, and seemingly effortlessly—both flow in, out, and among this expansive coffee bean field or vineyard. By actively striving to live life with an acquired taste, they consciously master themselves and enjoy each moment as it comes throughout this perpetually transcendent process of life.

In "A Match Made in (Whatever Your Belief System)," the light was graciously shined onto Miranda as she was in the spotlight. She was previously hiding in the shadows throughout most of the first part of *The 2650 Mile Aisle*, as chronologically it wouldn't make sense otherwise. Although when discussing Justin's character throughout "Part 1: Pre-Miranda," Miranda's name most often could have been used interchangeably, however she does possess subtle nuances which make Miranda, Miranda. Now with her warm welcoming complete, she has officially boarded the ship for the remainder of this voyage. We have learned that Miranda's intellect is second to none, and her sense of adventure doesn't trail far behind—having hiked the immense Rocky Mountains which were practically in her backyard while growing up. She enjoys reading a well-written novel as much as she savors visiting Mother Nature via hiking a multiple mile trail. Miranda's brilliance and sense of adventure drew Justin and her close together, but her irrefutable independence akin to that of Justin's was and is also a major factor in their harmonious relationship. Further, Justin and Miranda both share an *acquired taste*-like perspective towards life. This way of living life is one of noticing the finer things; it is one of simplicity; it is one of truth; it is one of purity; and it is one of being connected with the present moment. Together Justin and Miranda enjoy somewhat trivial activities—such as cooking dinner—as if it were the greatest thing that ever was. And in their eyes, I truly think they view every activity as the greatest activity that ever was. Before Justin and Miranda met, they both enjoyed all things unconditionally, but together this outlook multiplies exponentially and becomes ever more potent, powerful, and evidently beautiful. Whether they are deciding what to watch on television or preparing to hike the Pacific Crest Trail—they remain calm, composed, and positive—as they trust themselves, and more importantly believe in each other.

Whatever one's belief system may be, it is apparent that Justin and Miranda are a perfect match for each other. Where this match was made in Heaven, on Earth, by fate, by destiny, by the Universe, by sheer chance, or whatever else; it matters not now. What is important is that their paths crossed one another's and now they are together and ready to pledge their vows to each other in marriage. Like a key and a lock, Justin and Miranda are meant for each other. A large reason why I can affirmatively say that Justin and Miranda are willing to accept each other is because they have already accepted themselves entirely. To find someone that is confident, one must already embody confidence. To identify somebody that is independent, one must already understand independence. To recognize a person that is adventurous, one must have already unlocked adventure in their own being. And certainly, to be together with somebody else, one must already be together within themselves. Justin and Miranda truly embody the word *togetherness*. The dictionary definition of togetherness is "the state of being close to another person or other people."[1] They both are consciously aware that togetherness is a "state of being" — a state that needs to be actively realized each and every moment.

Walt Whitman is a prominent and timeless American poet of the 1800s who was a latter-day successor of Homer, Virgil, Dante, and Shakespeare. In his famous poem *Leaves of Grass*, he celebrated democracy, nature, love, and friendship.[2] "We Two Boys Together Clinging" is a beautiful passage from his poem that eloquently and indirectly states and describes Justin and Miranda's relationship with each other, and also themselves — as well as their way of being and living in general:

> *We two boys together clinging.*
> *One the other never leaving.*

> *Up and down the roads going, North and South excursions*
> > *making.*
> *Power enjoying, elbows stretching, fingers clutching.*
> *Arm'd and fearless, eating, drinking, sleeping, loving.*
> *No law less than ourselves owning, sailing, soldiering, thieving,*
> > *threatening.*
> *Misers, menials, priests alarming, air breathing, water drinking, on*
> > *the turf or the sea-beach dancing.*
> *Cities wrenching, ease scorning, statutes mocking, feebleness chas-*
> > *ing.*
> *Fulfilling our foray.*[3]

Together, Justin and Miranda stay clinging. And fulfilling their forays indeed they do.

CHAPTER 7: ADVENTURERS AT HEART

Living deep within Justin and Miranda's being is an overflowing abundance of adventure. It is an enjoyable itch that can never quite be scratched by either of them. Whether innately ingrained or not I do not know, but what I do know is that this adventurous and curious outlook and lifestyle has been attached to them for as long as they can remember. Asking Justin and Miranda to explain how they started their venturesome attitudes is like asking somebody to recall how he/she first learned to speak. Their ambitious and explorative mentalities have increasingly become stronger and more expansive over the years. Rather than exploring around the constraints of her backyard as a child, Miranda now hikes the Grand Canyon like it's a walk in the park. Rather than traveling to uncommonly visited local rope swings with his friends like Justin did in high school, he now strives to explore every single inch of the world. For instance, Miranda and Justin navigated across parts of Europe after they graduated college. Justin and Miranda do not travel and hike as a means to get away from the world or run from themselves. Instead, they venture to locations and trails far and wide to enhance the sense of adventure that is already inside of them. They appreciate the outdoors because it allows them to become more in-tuned with themselves, having no distractions. The experience of voyaging itself is worth all its value to them. Even in day-to-day activities, such as fishing, Justin and Miranda will treat their evening like it is a journey into the Amazon Rainforest—fascinated by the smallest of insects, to the largest of birds, to simply enjoying the still presence of Mother Nature herself.

Justin and Miranda, before they met, were no doubt exceedingly independent and enjoyed the outdoors and nature. But after they were together, their already heightened sense of adventure grew exponentially to unbelievable proportions. The more foreign the places that they traveled to—and the grander each location visited—the more they realized themselves. Before they boosted the magnitude of their crusades, Justin and Miranda unquestionably were comfortable with themselves and had an idea of who each of them represented on the inside. But once they completely escalated their journeys, their senses of themselves became progressively clearer, and they wholly realized who they truly were on the inside. Their true selves and sense of adventure became so apparent to them that they never thought about turning back—and actually started to push their limits of adventure even further.

Mother Nature opened Justin and Miranda's eyes to the all-embracing world in front of them. These two are intellectually gifted and sure of the opinions they harnessed, but when it comes to Mother Nature, they know they must submit and bow down as she is always right—and will win ten out of ten battles. Rather than futilely fighting against her, they work with Mother Nature instead. For example, Justin and Miranda went snowshoeing at near-zero temperatures in Colorado a couple of winters ago. Their egos didn't dissuade them that they would only need a few layers of clothing since they were already avid hikers. In lieu, they were amply suited with a sufficient amount of warm, light clothing layers that they could shed throughout the day. On top of that, Justin and Miranda remembered to bring an extra water supply as it is required to do so in higher elevations since water is lost through respiration twice as quickly at a high altitude than at sea level[1]—as Mother Nature can be unforgiving if not respected and does not care who crosses her path. She is the grand stage and Justin and Miranda are the actors in the play. It's evident there are varying degrees of creative genius in acting, and Justin and Miranda belong on Broadway. With their kayaking trips in the rivers of Michigan, to their nearly weeklong backpacking trip through the Grand Canyon, among numerous other pursuits—Justin and Miranda consciously recognized the grander scheme of Mother Nature and life in general. The vastness of the starry night sky in the Grand Canyon—which extended for what seemed like forever to them—made a flat tire look laughable. In a large part due to the outdoors, their potential full sense of adventure and discovery was actualized, and evidently, their sense of living was enhanced to its highest degree too. In nature, Justin and Miranda feel at home—fully aware of their inner and outer surroundings—connected as one with the Universe. Somehow, they have found a way to infiltrate this same sort of serenity and stillness granted by Mother Nature into their daily lives and activities as well—whether while at work or even cleaning the dishes after dinner—remaining present through it all.

In the famous piece of literature, *Walden*, Henry David Thoreau beautifully states, "My days were not days of the week, bearing the stamp of any heathen deity, nor were they minced into hours and fretted by the ticking clock; for I lived like the Puri Indians, of whom it is said that 'for yesterday, to-day, and to-morrow they have only one word, and they express the variety of meaning by pointing backward for yesterday, forward for to-morrow, and overhead for the passing day."[2] Mother Nature, even if for only glimpses initially, showed Justin and Miranda eternity.

Justin and Miranda view every single moment of every single day as an adventure. The feelings of curiosity we all had as young children have stuck with Miranda and Justin as they age. Instead of growing out of curiosity as the vast majority of people do, they have matured with curiosity—sharpening and igniting this characteristic more and more each and every day and each and every quest into the wilderness. Justin, although not huge on remembering quotes—as he prefers to live them—has repeatedly said, "Not all those who wander are lost."[3] I am unsure if he is even aware of the quote's origin— but regardless, it stuck to his heart. They say that curiosity killed the cat, so Justin and Miranda must not be felines, as they dive headfirst into uncertainty and come out unscathed. The unknown excites these two. Whether it is the uncertainty of what today has in store or the unpredictability of a fork in a trail that separates into two paths; they commit wholeheartedly to the path underneath their feet and don't look back. It is a gorgeously liberating way to live—to be comfortable and confident, and better yet enthralled with the unknown. In so many words that is what the pure essence of adventure is. Justin and Miranda—time and time again—have said that they "Work to live; not live to work." A saying like this can only genuinely come out of the mouths of two adventurers at heart.

CAMERON JAMES WILLIAMS

Broadening Their Horizon

After Justin and Miranda graduated from Case Western University, they decided to broaden their horizons by traveling to Europe. In their excursion, these explorers visited Munich, Nuremberg, Prague, Vienna, Budapest, Melk, and Salzburg. Justin and Miranda chose to travel through a variety of different locations to expand their palates as much as possible while they were overseas. Contrary to the average tourist—who was simply visiting another continent to take some nice pictures and say that they went somewhere—this trip to Europe held another meaning for Justin and Miranda. They wanted to experience each country and city as if they actually lived there. Instead of separating and regarding themselves as tourists relative to the native people, they made it a point to become one with the local community. Justin and Miranda slept in hostels most of their stay to truly experience each place as it actually was. They ate the local food, drank the local beverages, interacted with the local individuals in the community, and shied away from the commonly visited places that attract heavy tourism traffic. For a few days, Justin and Miranda imagined themselves as a couple who grew up in Prague, or as two individuals who have always lived in the Munich culture, and so on and so forth.

THE 2650 MILE AISLE

Justin, while in Vienna—to fully incarnate himself as a young Austrian man—took a swim in the Danube River which was located next to a giant castle. He flippantly mentioned how he forgot a towel but that was the least of his concerns as he felt the refreshing Austrian water submerge his body. And certainly, the fresh scent of the lush Viennese greenery at shore wiped any angst of not being able to dry off out of his mind.

An elegant, yet passionate depiction of the power of experience is found in the movie *Good Will Hunting*. Robin Williams, who plays a well-respected, veteran psychologist, proclaims to Matt Damon—who stars as a headstrong, brilliant young man who was an orphan from the South Boston—an iconic monologue of truth, asserting:

So if I asked you about art you'd probably give me the skinny on every art book ever written. Michelangelo? You know a lot about him. Life's work, political aspirations, him and the pope, sexual orientation, the whole works, right? But I bet you can't tell me what it smells like in the Sistine Chapel. You've never actually stood there and looked up at that beautiful ceiling. Seen that. If I asked you about women you'd probably give me a syllabus of your personal favorites. You may even have been laid a few times. But you can't tell me what it feels like to wake up next to a woman and feel truly happy. You're a tough kid. I ask you about war, and you'd probably, uh, throw Shakespeare at me, right? 'Once more into the breach, dear friends.' But you've never been near one. You've never held your best friend's head in your lap and watched him gasp his last breath, looking to you for help. And if I asked you about love you probably quote me a sonnet. But you've never looked at a woman and been totally vulnerable. Known someone could level you with her eyes. Feeling like God put an angel on Earth just for you...who could rescue you from the depths of hell. And you wouldn't know what it's like to be her angel to have that love for her to be there forever. Through anything. Through cancer. You wouldn't know about sleeping sitting up in a hospital room for two months holding her hand because the doctors could see in your eyes that the term 'visiting hours' doesn't apply to you. You don't know about real loss, because that only occurs when you love something more than you love yourself. I doubt you've ever dared to love anybody that much.[1]

Robin Williams' character recounted the events of his life to show the character of Matt Damon, who was his patient—as well as a genius—the extreme disparity between knowledge and experience.

It was one thing for Justin to look at pictures of the pristine river in Austria, but a completely different feeling was invoked when he experienced the river water for himself first-hand. Justin, a polar bear of sorts, takes the opportunity to swim in any new body of water he comes across—when camping, hiking, or any other activity—wherever

THE 2650 MILE AISLE

he can encounter a refreshing pool wash over his body for the first time.

Justin and Miranda share this 'search and appreciation of experience' character trait in anything they do, extending beyond just bodies of water and trips to other countries. With that being said, this discovery mentality was in full effect throughout their endeavors in Europe. Whether it was a homemade ale in Melk, or a bridge they crossed in Budapest, they treated every new happening as sacred—and etched it to their heart and souls. I vividly remember Justin and Miranda recounting their trip overseas when they returned home. The descriptions of their accounts painted the clearest picture in my family's and my own mind, as if we were actually with them in the hostel in Salzberg. Their environment was so precisely described that I could almost feel the warmth of the candle that they blew out one specific night before they fell asleep. They failed to miss a single detail in the verbal exposition of their escapade through Europe—from the distinct smell of the flowers in Prague to the sunset witnessed in Munich. The reason for their crystal-clear recollection was because they were completely and utterly alert every single moment while in Europe. Justin and Miranda strive to live this way in their day-to-day lives, but their conscious presence intensified being over 4,000 miles from home—or I should say their house—because the feeling of home is where Justin and Miranda are at any given moment. "Home is where the heart is" is interminably exemplified by Justin and Miranda beautifully.

    Justin and Miranda's trip to Europe planted a seed in their minds of how much there actually is to see and experience on this Earth. Their sense of adventure and discovery was prevalent prior to their travels out of the country, but the trip undoubtedly strengthened this already evident lifestyle. Ever since, they have continued to sow and tend to this planted seed, as every one of their journeys is grander—and perhaps more challenging—than the one prior. I reckon Justin and Miranda's quest to Europe was akin to pirates of the olden days searching for buried treasure. Except their reward wasn't gold; nor was the reward jewelry. Instead, they were on the pursuit for experience—and that's exactly what they received. On their voyage overseas, Justin and Miranda continued to push the limits of life—and broaden their horizons.

"Run, Justin (Forrest), Run"

Justin—as we've learned—was a lineman in his football days. The nature of a lineman is to have a more massive stature than anyone on the team to be able to push other large men with brute force either forward or backward. Justin, although not being the largest lineman in the locker room or field—was still rather substantial in size. Standing at around 6'1", Justin weighed approximately 250 pounds in his playing days. Although having lost weight after hanging up the cleats, he still weighed well over 200 pounds. In other words, Justin is not built for running. No doubt is Justin agile and athletic, but I wouldn't pick him first in a sprinting competition—and certainly not a long-distance running contest.

In 2017, the latter is exactly what he set out to accomplish—run the Detroit/Windsor International Half-Marathon. Justin has always sought out challenges to overcome—evidently progressing and leveling up in life—so this came as no surprise to me when I was informed of the new obstacle of growth that stood in his way. With Miranda's copious support, Justin began to train for the half-marathon months ahead of time. At least five days a week he would go for a trot around the neighborhood or at the gym—starting with three miles; then bumping up to five the next week, and then seven the following week, and so on and so forth until he was comfortably running thirteen miles.

Some people "run" half-marathons or full marathons just to say to others that they crossed the finish line—although walking portions of it—which is 100% okay. This is not the approach Justin took to the Detroit/Windsor International Half-Marathon. The saying goes "It's a marathon, not a sprint." With that being said, Justin viewed the thirteen miles as a race—not against the other individuals signed up—but against himself. He was competing against that voice inside his head that said, "You're getting tired, Justin. Slow down and take a break." Throughout his thirteen-mile adventure, that voice undoubtedly was speaking to him, tempting him to quit. But Justin was well aware that the only way was through; so he kept on running (and perhaps with his sense of humor remaining intact he said to himself "Run, Justin, run," echoing the legendary quote from the movie *Forrest Gump*). He was knowledgeable of the fact that the mind tends to quit well before the body shuts down. The half-marathon was absolutely a trial of physical stamina—but moreover—it was a test of mental endurance. Justin was conscious of this when signing up, and that's exactly the reason he embarked on the mission to begin with. He enjoyed the feeling of running, but it was more so another way to test his mental and physical abilities—and conquer himself.

THE 2650 MILE AISLE

And with his definitive purpose in mind the entire time, that's exactly what he accomplished — completing the Detroit/Windsor International Half-Marathon in 1 hour and 49 minutes, a little over an 8 minute/per mile pace. At the finish line, Miranda was there to greet her sweaty companion with open arms (and a bottle of water). She recognized and appreciated that he dashed the race wholeheartedly — as she would expect nothing less from him — because she would expect nothing less from herself in that situation. It was undeniably a memorable and inspirational feat, but Justin viewed it as another small step and crest of a hilltop in the grander mountain of life. Although Forrest Gump said, "Life is like a box of chocolates. You never know what you're going to get"[1] — Justin was 100% sure he would finish the half-marathon in a timely fashion — before the starting gun was even fired. The Detroit/Windsor International Half-Marathon was yet another manifestation of Justin's willingness to push the limits of himself, and of life; albeit this undertaking was a conscious choice, perhaps making it more astonishing.

    I have never personally run more than a 5k race. And no matter how many documentaries I watch or books I read on marathon runners or how to run marathons — I guarantee Justin has a better understanding of half-marathons than I do — because he has actually run one. I can also guarantee that throughout any barrier in life, when the negative voice of adversity inside of Justin's head says, "I have you cornered now buddy," he optimistically responds by saying to himself, "Run, Justin, run."

The Grand Proposal

Justin and Miranda's four to five-day hike through the Grand Canyon slightly under two years ago was the most significant event in both of their lives up until that point. The backpacking trip was the longest time frame and distance Justin and Miranda had dared to summon until then—arguably being the most challenging endeavor of their lives—but the traverse through the immense Grand Canyon held a more important meaning than simply an extensive hike. Both of their lives would be changed forever from that milestone onward. Graduating college was touted in high regards, as well as their adventure in Europe, but the journey through the canyon would take the cake as the most noteworthy of occurrences. And just as their international trek overseas, this experience was detailed in depth after the fact. Once again, my family and I were transmitted mentally to the Grand Canyon as if we were actually on the adventure ourselves. Not the slightest of a detail was omitted in this recap either. From the smell of the Arizonan flowers to the feeling of the fresh morning dew on their skin in the brisk early morning; every minute aspect was captured in their verbal recollection.

Well prepared with adequate food, shelter, and equipment, Justin and Miranda departed for the trailhead to begin the quest of their lives—but not before Justin received a blessing from Mr. and Mrs. Huiting beforehand. Justin and Miranda arrived at the trail, their home for the next four days. But before the commencement of their arduous journey, they rested in stillness for a few moments while looking out into the immeasurable magnitude of Mother Nature's creation before their eyes. Completely immersed and in awe of the surreal present moment they found themselves in, they gracefully took the first step of the rest of their lives.

  At the end of the first night and initial leg of the trail, Justin and Miranda arrived at a nearly indescribably beautiful crest that overlooked the vast Grand Canyon. Simultaneously, in a mesmerized gaze—both in and out of the canyon—they decided it would be the perfect place to rest up for the following day. As they were setting up camp—when the sun was just about to gently temporarily disappear into the horizon—Justin pulled Miranda aside. In a moment of pure bliss; of heart to heart; of soul to soul; of absolute togetherness with each other and Mother Nature—Justin knelt down on one knee and he told Miranda he wanted to spend the rest of his life with her. Her feelings reciprocated his and in a moment of utter jubilation she said "Yes," and they embraced each other. That enchanting sunset, which transcended the concepts of time and space, was the first one Justin and Miranda would be captivated by "officially" together—although that was already the case. That life-changing event would mark the end of one chapter of their lives and be the beginning of writing their new chapter as one. They were the authors of this book and they knew — although that what just happened was the most significant event up to that point — that the climax had yet to be reached in their adventurous story of life. Justin and Miranda showed us the first picture they snapped together after the proposal. There was pure elation illuminating from their faces as tears of joy glossed their eyeballs. It was a snapshot of pure bliss — but the moving feelings invoked by the picture surely dwarfed in size to how they actually felt — as that type of serenity is impossible to be captured second-hand. What better way of starting the most daunting hike of their lives than to be engaged?

While sitting in the dining room, Justin and Miranda continued their precise description of their venture into the wilderness; I could nearly feel the boundlessness of the Grand Canyon underneath my feet. I have never seen my brother as taken back, astonished, or humbled as he was by the grandness of the canyon he explored the week prior. The experience is one that will be engraved in Justin and Miranda's hearts forever, as even they were speechless recounting some of the breathtaking sites they saw. In one of Justin's uploaded pictures on social media of their day-by-day account of the trek, the impression of fascination seeped through the words in his caption. Justin, who usually when posting on social media is rather light-hearted and joking, approached this upload differently. Although there was a sprinkle of his usual wit, the caption in its entirety was rather serious, passionate, and poetic. Attached to the series of photos of the majestic Grand Canyon views there was a picture of a river winding through the crevasses, and obviously the excited caress of the newly engaged couple. Justin wrote:

> *A 2am start to our morning was by far the earliest but necessary as this would be our furthest leg of the loop. Mother Nature blessed us with another star/moonlit start. We encountered a rather intimidating scorpion that blocked our path along the way. I would've liked to say I wasn't puckered up tighter than a duck's ass... but that was not the case. Nonetheless we paid our toll and he let us pass. As the stars began to fade and the sky brightened, the path led us to a lookout point with views of the river and vast plateaus of rock surrounding us entirely. The feeling of standing there in a land of nothing next to my everything is a moment tough to describe yet impossible to forget. The energy amidst stillness, the world going on up there while we were in complete solitude down here. We took another step in our journey together, gathering two more rocks along the way... 1 for Miranda's hand and 1 for our adventure rock collection. We reached camp early enough to enjoy the day as a newly engaged couple. Camp was quite the 5-star resort*

coming from the more primitive sites from the days prior. We capped off the day of celebration with a 5.5 oz flask of 95-degree rum.

One thing Justin kept saying regarding one of the sites seen while Miranda and he were rehashing their adventure was "It was like a painting." As he described the awe-inspiring view of the Grand Canyon he couldn't go one sentence without saying "It was like a painting," almost in disbelief of the dreamlike experience Miranda and he absorbed the previous week. Justin's most extreme admiration of Mother Nature was manifested by those five words, as he surrendered himself with complete gratitude and trust to the workings of the Universe that he couldn't quite comprehend. Miranda was just as dumbfounded by the beauty of the seemingly infiniteness of Mother Nature's creation, as they both agreed there weren't words that served justice to the magnificence of the Grand Canyon. The views, hike, and engagement in the Grand Canyon is a week Justin and Miranda will never forget and always hold dear to their cores, as it marked the formal beginning of their new journey through this life together. The memories of their experience of that specific trek through the Grand Canyon are sure to last a lifetime—as who could possibly forget the sights of the purest of all vistas—as well as the grand proposal?

CAMERON JAMES WILLIAMS

Welcome to Pure Michigan

A little over a year ago, my dad and I visited Justin and Miranda for a weekend at their apartment in Novi, Michigan. We toted our kayaks on top of my dad's Civic, excited to get on new waters with Justin and Miranda, as well as for the first time see where they were living. Upon our arrival at the apartment complex, we were greeted in the parking lot by a shirtless Justin (he was always shirtless) and a clothed Miranda. As we were catching up and loosening up our car legs, Justin and Miranda gave my dad and me an in-depth tour of their bunker. Immediately upon entering the abode I was astonished of how organized their two-bedroom place was. For not being a very large apartment, it was spacious yet had an unbelievable amount of their belongings stashed somewhere precisely. The one bedroom was strategically arranged to be the home for all their outdoor supplies—from kayaks to bikes, and tents to snowshoes—most of which were stored in a wooden shelf built from scratch by Justin. Not an inch of space was wasted, and after a couple of bikes and oars were moved into the other bedroom, an air mattress was blown up for my dad and me. I initially thought the open concept of their living quarters was coincidental, but surely it was selected to be that way, as I could feel the pleasantness and intent in every room.

We made our way to the kitchen to finish the official *MTV Cribs*-esque tour. To no surprise, every single thing had a specific place and served an exact purpose there too. The simplest of items were deliberately and delightfully orchestrated for the fullest, most enhanced experience for the two of them—and any potential visitors. Justin and Miranda stored as many of their food items as possible in mason jars to save space and preserve freshness. It's little things, like how they stored coconut flakes in mason jars for preservation and space-saving purposes to thriftily using a water filter jug instead of buying bottled water, that impressed me. But that was just the beginning of their thoughtful and conscious nuances in their apartment. The coffee table in their living room was decorated with hand-made art courtesy of Miranda as well as quick reads that would brighten anyone's—including their guests'—day.

My dad and I were led out to their back porch which sat fifteen yards from the shore of a pond. I could tell that is where they spent most of their time—not only because of the rocking chairs stationed on the concrete patio—but because water and land critters large and small pervaded the vicinity. From a beautiful white swan sitting still in the middle of the pond to the hummingbirds persistently flapping before our eyes—and then disappearing only to return again—the Earth rested in silence as we perched on the porch for a few moments, but which felt like eternity. A fish,

THE 2650 MILE AISLE

respecting the swan's personal space, jumped out of the pool for an instant to say hello and then returned to the depths of the water. As dusk was around the corner, the bullfrogs started to sing to us in unison by the edge of the water, taking turns leading the symphony, and then granting the duty to another one of their own. In the faint distance, I could hear a solo crow making his presence known, informing us down on the ground that there was an eye in the sky protecting us. I unconsciously said to myself, "This is like a painting" as we inhaled our last few breaths of pure Michigan air before returning back inside. Just as we were sliding open the door, Justin called out, "Hey Greg" as I anticipated their next-door neighbor was outside too. Unexpectedly, it was a crane gently and definitively passing by, only ten or so yards from us. "Where's Judy?" Miranda genuinely asked, as I pieced together that must have been Greg's mate. It dawned on me that instead of Justin and Miranda viewing the birds as guests to their complex—it was the other way around—and they assumed the utmost respect and appreciation for their hosts.

    The next morning, we woke early to the delicious smell of scrambled eggs and freshly ground French Press coffee to get a head start on our day filled with adventure. As I wiped the grogginess from my eyes and brushed my teeth for the day, the table was being set by Justin and Miranda—like it was clockwork—timing out the meal flawlessly. The effort and tenderness they infused into the eggs and toast was noticeable, as they made such a simple dish taste so incredibly extravagant; but how foolish of me to expect anything different from them. Justin was eager to present to our dad and me a sampler platter of some of his artisan-like tea collection. He unscrewed the mason jars and steeped a few bags for us—setting a timer—because as I learned that weekend, black and green tea steep for different amounts of time and require particular temperatures of water. You would have thought he was carrying the original Declaration of Independence over to the dining table, as he cautiously and graciously set the herbal teas in front of us. And of course, he insisted that we at least taste the tea first before adding sugar or honey. Justin was thrilled to discuss the varying flavor profiles and layered accents of the exotic teas. It was as if at that moment in time the only thing on his mind was the cup of tea in his hand—because I believe that was actually the case—as he sipped the tea like he was experiencing it for the first time. After our Michigan Tea Party, Justin and Miranda informed us that the next day's unique morning-beverage was slated to be cold brew coffee, as it necessitated preparation a period ahead of time. Justin took care of that while Miranda finished up making our lunches we would enjoy while on the water.

With fuel in our tank, my dad and I helped haul their kayaks out of our make-shift bedroom.

THE 2650 MILE AISLE

Watching Justin and Miranda strap the boats to their car was worth the trip enough. It was like watching a ballerina flow with her favorite song, or Leonardo Da Vinci constructing his flying machine. Whatever the case, it was an absolute art-form observing them secure the kayaks to their vehicle. Miranda, as I learned that weekend, could compete in the Olympics for professional knot tying if there was such a thing. Justin hoisted the first kayak on the car and then Miranda diligently and swiftly entered a zone as she did a loopity-loop and pull here, and another one there—and by that time her hands were moving so quickly that I couldn't keep track of the course of the rope as it transformed into a knot. By the time Justin lifted the other kayak on the car she was already eagerly awaiting him, so she could work her magic connecting the other boat to the car (I'm not sure if even Houdini could have escaped one of her knots). They were like a machine, and before my dad and I knew it we were on our way to the Huron River.

    The currents were relentless that day, and it was imperative to have some skill, finesse, and experience kayaking. Fortunately, it wasn't my dad or my first foray on choppy waters—but was undoubtedly the most challenging waters we've paddled in thus far. Justin and Miranda led the way, since they were well aware of and seasoned in that specific river, and because it was in their blood to do so. When approaching exceedingly rapid currents, I distinctively recall Justin saying to not hesitate in the rapids, but to "Paddle through them." Justin and Miranda were well aware that through the rough currents of life and unpromising, uncontrollable happenings throughout it that the only way was through. To this day when faced with a hardship or an unpredictable waterway, I often remind myself that the most effective and time-tested route is to paddle through.

With our latissimus dorsi muscles sore from paddling and stomachs filled with tasty sandwiches—and hearts overflowing with adventure—we returned back to Justin and Miranda's port just before dark. I jumped in the shower and like clockwork, once again, the 'old-fashioned' adult beverages were conscientiously being prepared, with exact measurements to the T of the proper volume. The recipe called for a certain amount of bourbon and bitter so that's exactly how it was concocted—nothing more and nothing less. The beverages were exquisitely served over an ice ball, in which Justin and Miranda owned the mold specifically for 'old-fashioned' cocktails when they would indulge in them. The elegance was able to be tasted in the glass—as my palate viewed it as a finer sip—and I could feel the passion instilled into the drink rush through my veins. I lounged on the couch while enjoying the engaging conversations and cocktail, and it was a cherry on top to the wonderful day.

THE 2650 MILE AISLE

  The next day Justin and I sat on the back porch and enjoyed the fresh air before my dad and I departed back to Pennsylvania. We waved hello to Greg and Judy and were talking about whatever thoughts flowed through our minds at that particular moment. I was always tantalized by how Justin kept a calm head through the toughest of situations in life. The conversation guided us to the topic of anxiety. Without beating around any bush, I directly asked him, "How don't you get anxiety?" curious to see his perspective on the matter. Without pausing for more than a second, he powerfully and succinctly said, "I just don't think about it." Our topic of conversation floated onto something else as we sat connected with Mother Nature. Shortly after, I gestured so-long to Greg and Judy—taking one last gander at the pond and the swan still gliding around on top of it—then Justin and Miranda helped my dad and I lug our bags to the car. We hugged and said our "See ya soons," and got on the highway. It was a marvelous weekend—from start to finish—and the hospitality of Justin and Miranda was spectacular. I will never forget Justin's response to the question by the pond; nor our experience on the Huron River; as well as the herbal teas; and the 'old-fashioned' beverage—as pure Michigan absolutely welcomed my dad and me with open arms.

CAMERON JAMES WILLIAMS

No Plan B

As mentioned previously in "The Announcement," the Williams family and one Huiting (not for long at this point) trekked the West Coast for a summer vacation. No one had ventured to California until that point, so we were all eager to experience the most western state in the United States underneath our feet. Prior to officially booking the trip there was a vote between Washington and California as the vacation destination point. Immediately upon agreeing that the final two spots were set, Justin and Miranda—within the next hour—created a descriptive weeklong itinerary of activities for both places. It was literally more informative than a paid Travelocity schedule. I'm not kidding. In only one hour, Justin and Miranda concocted options of places to stay, places to eat, choices for rental cars, passes that would need to be purchased; and a slew of activities in each specific region we would stay, and then some. They did this same exact detailed draft of an itinerary for both Washington and California. After seeing a trifurcated setup of the California option—starting at San Francisco, then traveling to Yosemite, and concluding the trip in Lake Tahoe—the unanimous decision was California. It was official. California is where we would vacation, following Justin and Miranda's professionally executed and precise itinerary. My

THE 2650 MILE AISLE

older sister cautiously noted the bus passes that needed to be purchased to hike the trail in Yosemite were on delay. She was inquiring what we would alternatively substitute that day if the hike didn't work out. Justin frankly texted back in our group message, "There's no plan B."

There was nothing but sunshine as the plane landed in San Francisco, as well in all three places enjoyed throughout our endeavors. Everyone was eager to locate our luggage revolving on the carousel, grab an In-N-Out burger or two, a bottle of Californian wine (dry, obviously), and jam out to some Eagles together as we traveled on the sun-kissed glistening highway to the Airbnb we would stay for the next two nights. I'm sure if the Eagles were in their prime today they would have named their famous allegorical song "Airbnb California" instead of "Hotel California," but obviously that's not the case, and certainly the deeper meaning of the song wouldn't apply here regardless. The place was an hour or two away from the airport, but time doesn't exist on vacation. We will revisit the first night in San Francisco in the next section, as more light will be shed on the announcement from Justin and Miranda that took place that night.

With that being said, the second day in San Francisco was one out of a movie. At the crack of dawn, my dad, brother, and I woke up our bodies, minds, and souls (although they never really sleep) with a 6 AM yoga class. As the sun was rising, we walked the half-mile to the studio and warmed our muscles up for the day ahead. It was a studio like we've never seen before and certainly one we will never forget. The instructor was connected to a microphone, and as we elongated in downward-facing dog pose with our eyes shut, it felt like she was speaking to me only—as the surround sound vibrated and resonated from every possible angle. My dad and Justin felt the same way as we reflected on the class afterward on our walk to the local coffee shop. Before the trip, we never knew what it was like to do yoga in California. That is not the case anymore.

As we returned to the Airbnb, everyone else was packing their bags for the day ahead as we would go explore Muir Woods. We all had previously seen Redwood Trees in movies and pictures online, but as we hopped out of the car and walked towards the trailhead everyone was speechless. Like the Grand Canyon, pictures don't serve justice to the magnificence and grandness of the Redwoods. We were going to spend the day with them, and they would show us their home. As our family hiked among their family—with our stillness matching their stillness—we ascended up the mountain as Justin and Miranda took the lead. At the end of the five miles, we found ourselves back at the lodge, and everyone wasn't quite exhausted—but actually refreshed—and it felt like we all had the energy to hike five days instead; however, other activities awaited us patiently. I am

THE 2650 MILE AISLE

certain that some of the strength of the roots and sturdiness of the trunks of the Redwoods were gifted to us by them—as we all walked back to the car, standing erect with smiles ear to ear on our faces. Our day and vacation were just beginning.

We ventured to a scenic spot overlooking the Golden Gate Bridge and stayed there for a while. On the car ride over, which felt like minutes—but could have very well been an hour—we all sang and danced to songs which we had never heard before. I'm sure we were perceived as buffoons by passing cars, but that was not a thought anywhere close to anyone's head as we performed our makeshift dance routine; a hybrid to the likes of the Backstreet Boys and the Jackson 5, with a healthy scoop of silliness. I remember the car ride more clearly than the famous Golden Gate Bridge.

After visiting the bridge—there were still a few hours of daylight left—so we headed for a beach on the Pacific Ocean. To no surprise, Justin couldn't wait more than three minutes to dive headfirst into the crashing waves of the Pacific Ocean. He and I bodysurfed waves until our appetite was fulfilled. It was the first time either of us had submerged in the Pacific Ocean which made it even more refreshing. Since the sun was starting to fade, and the temperature wasn't by any means warm—the locals stayed on the sand—as Justin and I were the only human souls in the water (Oh, how alive and inviting was Mother Nature and her perpetual pool that day!) Justin and I dried off, laid on the beach with our family for a while longer, and then we all drove back to the Airbnb to socially sip the wine which gracefully rested on the table until our arrival.

Before the sun had completely risen the next day, we were already on our way to Yosemite National Park. As we were warmed up from Muir Woods the day prior, we were ready to pursue the ten-mile adventure through Yosemite National Park. When driving through the winding roads of the mountainous and rocky forest, our car must've looked like a crawling ant to the enormous mountains above our heads. But every ant has its purpose—and ours was to hike ten miles together through a place we had never experienced. Yosemite National Park is so vast and immense that a bus is required to drop hikers off at the correct trailhead. There was no plan B that day as Justin and Miranda managed to secure bus tickets for everyone a week before our trip out west. Up the mountain we were hauled as our bus driver was more akin to a tour guide. He discussed anything imaginable relating to Yosemite National Park—from its history; to record-holding rock climbers, such as Alex Honnold; to specific trees living there; as well as sliding in a subtle joke here and there that seemingly only Justin and I were amused by, because most people were sleeping from the early rise (Gus appreciated us, and we

THE 2650 MILE AISLE

appreciated him). The extensive, informative bus ride was a perfect way to start our ten-mile journey.

Alex Honnold, who Gus enlightened us of, is an American rock climber best known for his solo ascents. He is the first individual to accomplish a free solo climb of El Capitan, which towers 7,569 feet above sea level and 3,600 feet above the valley. Honnold completed this magnificent feat in 2017.[1] Thirty-one people have died attempting to scale the granite behemoth,[2] and he is the first one to ever to conquer it without a rope attached. When Honnold set out to accomplish his goal, there was no turning back—as his life was clenched on the rocks beneath his fingertips. Free solo rock climbers push their limits to the nth degree because there is absolutely no room for error when facing nature. The less space for slippage, the more engaged the individual must be. Rock climbing amplifies this truth to the highest extreme because it is literally a life or death situation. I'm sure that is partially what attracts these courageous individuals to the sport; the unknown, the overcoming and mastering of fears and risks inherent with it, the precision in execution, the 'no turn back' mentality, and the sense of presence and peace becoming connected as one with a massive rock and evidently Mother Nature. It is a bold task, but the reward lasts a lifetime for these brave souls—and is not something that can be stolen or taken away.

As we reached the trailhead, the bus came to a halt and Gus informed us it was okay to exit the greyhound. We thanked Gus for more than just the service he provided, and as we stepped foot off the bus, an overwhelming feeling washed over me, and I'm sure everyone else there too. Justin and Miranda immediately simultaneously scurried to a ledge overlooking the valley underneath—as there were miles upon miles of mountain ahead, and an infinite blue sky up above. After a quick restroom break, we started our ten-mile quest, yet our adventure was already well underway. The sights seen, and splendor they embodied, were indescribable. We paused every so often to embrace the fresh air and creation we were encircled in; the mountains, boulders, and waterfall spewing over the cliff across the valley truly looked like a painting.

      Eventually, our hike's route horse-shoed around the valley and we arrived at the waterfall we were astonished at an hour earlier. Of course, Justin and Miranda peeked over the ledge to get a better look at the empty abyss full of wildlife and trees thousands of feet below, as the water sprayed its substance down onto them. Only yards ahead of the cliff and waterfall rested a pool of frigid water consisting of the melted snow from the previous winter. Every year—long before anyone even was aware of it—the snow melted creating the stream and waterfall that existed before our eyes. As I was taking a sip of water and looked to my right, Justin's left boot and sock were off, and he was already working on the right one. It didn't take a rocket scientist to know what would happen next. Before I could blink, his shirt was off and he was floating in Mother Nature's ice-cold king-size bathtub. He let himself submerge in the water, washing the liquid over his face and hair as if he was getting baptized. But undoubtedly, he felt renewed after every new sea of water he dipped in, and the same went for any one that wasn't new. Justin tied his boots back onto his feet and we continued our exploration through the grand Yosemite National Park. As we reached the bottom of the valley, the skyline turned an orange and purplish hue as the sun was ready to dive back behind the trees and recharge for its next rise. We followed suit and returned to the Airbnb to bask in the California evening before heading to Lake Tahoe the following day.

Our plans were to experience the Nevada portion of Lake Tahoe, so our lengthy trip demanded us to depart early in the morning. But when the feeling of togetherness and peace of mind is prevalent, traveling any distance is surmountable, and actually congenial. We arrived in our Lake Tahoe Airbnb for the last leg of the trip. We wasted zero time as kayaking on Lake Tahoe was our adventure for the day. It was a gorgeous day and the sun was shining bright—not that it mattered—and we waited in line to rent the kayaks. The water in Lake Tahoe was crystal-clear, and it felt like we were the first human beings ever to inhabit the lake. Peering off into the distance at the edge of the lake was the Sierra Nevada, with their peaks still glistening with snow. We continued to gently paddle away from the shore. For the considerable amount of time we were paddling ahead in the immeasurable pool of water, when gazing forward it seemed like we weren't going anywhere—but only until glancing behind us did we realize the substantial progress being made. Somewhere in the middle of the lake was the Nevada/California border, as the end of one state signals the beginning of another. Looking at a topographical map, it would appear there is a divide in the middle of Lake Tahoe—but the lake felt like one single body of water that day, undivided and all-encompassing.

As we returned to shore just in time before our rented session expired, we placed the kayaks back in their proper positions for the next fortunate explorers. The gentleman at the station enlightened us that the deepest point of the lake was over 1,600 feet. We were baffled at how a lake so clear—and at the surface seeming rather shallow—could be so incredibly deep. We thanked him for his kayak rental and fun fact, as we were also expressing gratitude for enabling the wonderful experience we just had and were having.

Day two in Lake Tahoe was a beach day—according to Justin and Miranda's itinerary—and my family was ecstatic. All our legs were sore from the hikes the previous days, and our back and shoulders were feeling tender from the kayak

THE 2650 MILE AISLE

expedition the day prior. Laying on the warm sand of a Lake Tahoe beach and drinking an adult beverage was the perfect icing on the cake to our Western excursion. Positive vibes and good conversations were on the menu for the day. And that's exactly what we indulged in. After laying on the beach for a couple of hours, Justin led the charge into Lake Tahoe to cool down. We all joined him and soaked up the crystal-clear pool, as the warmth of the sun and the coolness of the water created a harmonious balance. In usual Justin fashion, the idea of swimming out to the buoy flashed in Justin's mind. With his invitation to me on the surface of the pristine water, I accepted it as I concluded that I may never have the chance to swim out to a buoy in Lake Tahoe with my brother ever again, and certainly that moment was as perfect as any. To this day I am glad Justin's courage washed onto me, as it was an experience I thoroughly enjoyed and will never forget.

    The entire West Coast excursion was phenomenal from start to finish. Frankly, an entire book could be written on the first-hand encounters, as simply a highlight reel was mentioned here. More seemingly trivial—and at the surface underwhelming, yet actually overwhelming—topics could have been discussed; such as the passion invoked into Justin and Miranda's home-made steak dinner relished on the back porch of the Airbnb in Yosemite (or even the more delightful conversations had on that same back porch); or the blackberries and raspberries picked on the side of the narrow Californian mountain ledged road; or the stillness of the San Francisco stars at night, twinkling as if to say hello; or the improv band jamming in the park we happened upon also in San Francisco; and the list of intricate, yet potent details goes on. Justin and Miranda embody the balance between calculation and spontaneity, and the week on the west coast solidified that. From executing their planned schedule exactly, to stumbling upon the Ghirardelli chocolate headquarters, we all received a true taste of California. Justin and Miranda's itinerary started as a thought in their brain and then was actively manifested into reality. Thanks to it and Justin and Miranda's willingness to push the envelope of the so-called traditional vacations—as well as themselves and their lives in general—our family and I enjoyed the trip of our lives as we all experienced the West Coast for the first time. Nothing less than this type of adventure was expected by Justin and Miranda, and in the wise words of Justin, "There's no plan B."

The Announcement (Again)

Before we officially leave the West Coast, the announcement, presented there by Justin and Miranda must be revisited. As we learned in the beginning pages of *The 2650 Mile Aisle*, in San Francisco, Justin and Miranda announced to our family how they would quit their jobs and hike the Pacific Crest Trail as a substitute for a traditional wedding. When we arrived at our Airbnb in San Francisco, everyone unpacked their belongings and each of us guided our own tours around the various rooms in the house. After looking around upstairs (placing dibs on bedrooms), surveying the front porch as well as the back, and everything in between (and Justin sarcastically shouting that the owners left food for us in the fridge to eat) — we all sat down on the couches in the living room, releasing one of those partial sighs and partial grunts that are inevitable after flying on a plane for over four hours (that's right you know, one of those "ooouuaahhhwww" sounds).

There was still some sunlight remaining in the day, so we decided as a family to follow the itinerary and walk through downtown San Francisco to experience the city first hand. After navigating through Chinatown, we found ourselves at Alcatraz Island. The sun was starting to fade into the water, so we savored the last couple bites of creamy clam chowder that a few minutes prior was overflowing the bread bowl it rested in. After that, we returned to the Airbnb to recharge for the exciting week ahead. As previously mentioned earlier in "The Announcement," my dad, Alexa, Abbey, and I caught wind that there was some sort of announcement that Justin and Miranda had planned, but ultimately, we were oblivious to the actual purpose of it. We continued to speculate guesses anyways.

    Now better acquainted with our Airbnb and the setup of the place, we each headed to our rooms to throw some pajamas on (Justin took his shirt off) and congregated back in the kitchen and living room area. After everyone was settled comfortably, Justin and Miranda glanced at each other and gave one of those "Let's do it now" signals with their eyes. At that moment, Justin and Miranda officially gathered us in one central location. As we huddled in the living room with our undivided attention granted to Justin and Miranda, they unhesitatingly dove headfirst into the announcement; the hiking of the Pacific Crest Trail in the coming spring and summer instead of a traditional wedding celebration. They explained their plans from start to finish without missing a single detail. Eventually, after an initial sense of bewilderment, a rush of inspiration washed over me as they precisely described their intentions and reasoning of embarking on the journey of a lifetime—intensely believing every word that exited their mouths. They clearly spelled out the dangers, risks, and uncertainties inherent of the exploration, but there was not an iota of doubt with their choice, and their decision had been immovably solidified in their minds. Just as Horatius collapsed the bridge behind him and battled diligently to defend Rome; and Alex Honnold had no choice to turn back and quit when scaling El Capitan—Justin and Miranda were bravely and utterly confident in their well-thought-out commitment of setting off to undertake the Pacific Crest Trail.

Later that evening—after popping a bottle of wine to celebrate their decision and life in general—Justin and I found ourselves in the same room together and he appreciated the stamp of approval his younger brother gave him regarding his fiancée and his courageous quest. Infatuated by the pleasant surprise, I inquired into when the thought of doing such a thing initially sparked into either Miranda or his brain. I was curious as to how the entire decision to choose such an unconventional path transpired. He explained everything as best he could, but I was conscious of the fact that a resolution like that is nearly indescribable—and that words can only attempt to concretize such a meaning and locate the source of the true intangible reason inside. I briefly digressed, and we continued our chat man to man; brother to brother; and heart to heart. This was one of those heart-to-heart conversations where both parties leave themselves completely vulnerable and let truth flow out of their mouths. Those are truly beautiful moments when the ego is nonexistent.

After a few more minutes we circled back to the topic on the forefront of both of our minds, the Pacific Crest Trail. Justin wasn't by any means second-guessing himself or Miranda and his decision, but he certainly was weighing all the potential dangers immanent of the trail. From mountain lions to bears, and hypothermia to heatstroke, and dehydration to insulin (since he's diabetic), as well as many other unpredictable challenges from Mother Nature—Justin surfaced all the risks. In a matter of fact way, he was aware of the fear that was within him facing such an obstacle, but even more so he was aware of how to overcome it. Justin explained an array of 'if, then, because' scenarios but knew deep down that every situation could not be predicted exactly—and at times he was going to need to rely on the only thing in his control; his reaction. He didn't avoid his fears; rather he faced them and focused on what was in his control and power.

At a point in our exchange of words, as he was dissecting every aspect of the trail, I felt a sense of hesitance in Justin for the first time ever. At first, I thought about agreeing with him, but then I realized that would only worsen any angst and add fuel to the fire. But just as he had guided me to the higher road many times through observations of his actions and character in life, it was my time to give back to him. It was my duty to take a positive approach and realign him away from any sort of negative thinking. At that moment, I frankly expressed how inspired I was about their decision. I confidently continued to say that if any two people were cut out for the task that lay ahead, it was surely Miranda and him. After all the positivity he has shed onto me over the years—whether knowingly or not—it was my calling to do the same for him in that moment (Oh, the gift that keeps on giving!) Justin and I carried on our trail conversation a little while longer and then started to talk about a variance of topics, such as the week ahead and how delicious the In-N-Out burgers were. We ventured out to the rest of the family in the dining room, passed the wine bottle around to finish the last drops, and soon after we all called it an early night as we had an adventurous vacation planned ahead of us.

CAMERON JAMES WILLIAMS

The Bracelet

Alright, I lied. Actually, one more thing is required to be mentioned and surfaced before we officially leave the West Coast. This seemingly trivial occurrence has subtly impressed a world of impact on my life. The occasion happened the day after Justin and Miranda made their announcement in San Francisco. Miranda was wearing a bracelet around her wrist that a close friend of hers made for her the year prior. She mentioned it was attached to her wrist for the entire spring and summer because she didn't feel the need to take it off. For some reason, as my family and I huddled in the dining room after an exhaustive day of adventure—after her enlightening me of the origin of the bracelet—she removed it from her wrist and granted it onto mine. I didn't think much of it at the time and perceived it as nothing more than a kind gesture.

Later that evening, while laying down in bed before falling asleep, the question flashed in my mind: "Was there a deeper significance to Miranda parting ways with a bracelet that she wore for so long?" The imaginative side of me wondered if she was granting me magical powers or casting some sort of spell on me. Obviously, I came to my senses quickly and let that thought flow through me like a breeze passing through a wired fence. Shortly after, a wave of gratitude, contentment, and pure joy washed over me, and then I fell asleep. I traditionally do not sport any sort of jewelry, watch, or bracelet on my wrist, as to me, it feels uncomfortable. The next morning, the bracelet was still on my wrist, although it didn't even feel like it at that point because I was already *used* to it. As it was already discussed, the vacation was one for the books due to all the unique experiences and exhilarating activities—but it certainly was not because of the bracelet. The experiences of the West Coast came and went, but the feeling of inspiration and sense of living remained with me.

As *normal* life resumed, I was grateful for the reset of sorts from the vacation out to the West. Back on the East, it felt as if I was more engaged and active in life than I ever was before. A couple of weeks passed, and the bracelet was still on my wrist as I didn't pay much mind to it, since I was more than *used* to it at that point. A month passed, and the bracelet was still circled around my left wrist. It's somewhat ironic because striving to maintain an understanding and lifestyle of nonattachment ranks in high regard to me, so I was not holding onto the memories made out westward. Instead, it was a reminder of the thing that knows no bounds. It was a reminder of a certain feeling that is difficult to attach words to. It was a reminder of freedom and courage. It was a reminder of confidently facing the unknown of the present moment. It was a reminder to push the limits of life. It was a reminder of progress. And evidently, it was a reminder of Justin and Miranda.

Delving deeper below the surface it became completely obvious to me that truth and meaning are on a sliding scale together. Truth signifies essentially nothing until a human being is involved. Consequently, a human being then extracts and invokes meaning from truth. Sometimes, truth and meaning do not always go hand in hand. Sometimes, it is beneficial to sacrifice a degree of truth if a greater sense of meaning is the result (or vice versa). For instance, the meaning and truth discussion is blatantly obvious in various parables as well as children's fables, to name only two particulars. For example, in *The Tortoise and the Hare*; no, obviously there was not a legitimate race between two animals. No, the hare didn't actually race far ahead off of the start and then become sidetracked, while the tortoise methodically progressed forward—and won the race. But these completely made-up symbols possess a deeper layer of meaning and inherent truth attached to them. It is not true that a tortoise and a hare raced; but, yes, it is true—and more importantly meaningful—that there is value and significance to human beings in the saying, "Slow and steady wins the race."

The same relevance of meaning is proved in the parable of *The Good Samaritan* from the Bible. In summary, the parable describes how there was a potentially Jewish traveler, who people just had robbed and beaten, leaving him on the road. A priest and another religious figure walked past him but ignored the man. Finally, a Samaritan passing by stopped to help the brutally beaten and injured man. He didn't care about race or religion, although Samaritans were known to despise Jews. The traveler eventually revealed himself as Christ.[1] Obviously, this story is not coated in utmost truth. With that being said, the moral of the parable is to unconditionally help anyone that is in need—an extremely powerful message that invokes a world of meaning. In this case as well, a layer of truth is required to be surrendered to impart and enhance the underlying meaning to us human beings.

  Today, the bracelet gifted from Miranda continues to remain on my wrist. Am I superstitious? Absolutely not. Do I think I will get struck by lightning if I take the bracelet off? Or that the house will burn down? Or that I will get hit by a bus while crossing the street? Of course not; that is outrageous to believe. Do I view the bracelet as a good luck charm? Or believe that it has superpowers? Once again, no.

  But here's what I do believe and know to be true: It is a reminder of Justin and Miranda and any time I meditate or reflect on the bracelet; or feel anxious and glance down at the bracelet; or start to lose confidence in myself and feel the bracelet on my wrist—a rush of inspiration and positive feelings wash over me like the tide of the ocean spreading gently over the shore. The presence of the bracelet helps to provide a necessary perspective shift and boost for me in any given moment of doubt or uncertainty. The feelings I feel are as real as ever. Although the actual bracelet is merely an emblem and issues no tangible effect, its intangible effect ultimately leads to a tangible result—as the intangible always precedes the tangible—just as the external world is permanently a reflection of our inner selves. At times, I am perfectly okay with sacrificing a level of truth to, in turn, attain an elevated sense of meaning which is as real as can be to me, and viably more influential.

Realistically, even when a bracelet is not on my wrist, these same exact feelings of inspiration and life are already latent inside of me waiting to be actualized—and unquestionably accessible and attainable. But as of right now, wearing the bracelet is a symbol and a reminder of the transcendent portal that is forever available inside of me, and you, bracelet or not. And perhaps the bracelet will be soon be passed on to a worthy, or should I say any, soul. No matter what its fate is or wherever the bracelet finds its next home, there is an absolute truth: Deathless is the symbolic meaning of the bracelet.

Planning for the PCT

As to be expected with the approximately six-month hike of the PCT, or Pacific Crest Trail, there is quite extensive planning necessary. Justin and Miranda were well aware of this and took the responsibility in stride, as they were more than conscious of the 'winning the battle before the fighting even starts' mentality. There was quite a bit of unpredictability in quitting their jobs to hike in the bare wilderness for half of a year—for example; finding a new job upon their return, facing the desert heat, dangerous animals, hypothermia, chance of drowning, etc. But what was in their control—such as applying for the trail permit, food supply, and equipment supply—remained within their reach of power.

    The first item on their vast checklist of preparation for the quest of the Pacific Crest Trail was receiving the required permits to even be allowed on the trail. As the permits for the Pacific Crest Trail are in limited supply, it is a first-come, first-served basis; so the acquisition of two permits for Justin and Miranda was not at all guaranteed. Although alert of this concerning fact, they remained unmoved and didn't worry about it, because it was simply a matter of the fact and out of their control. But what was in their authority was applying for the trail permits at the earliest possible time. That is exactly what they did. On the earliest possible day—wait no, hour... wait, actually minute—they were on the website ready to click the button to apply for the permits. Once that button was clicked, it was out of their hands, and Justin and Miranda were assured that they put their best foot forward. To their delight, a week or two later they received a notice from the Pacific Crest Trail Association that the applications were reviewed and that their permits would be sent in the mail shortly. Justin and Miranda were thrilled as they were officially going to embark on the journey of their lives. By receiving the required permits for the Pacific Crest Trail, Justin and Miranda were certainly lucky—if there is such a thing.

At that point in time, the permits were checked off of Justin and Miranda's hefty preparatory laundry list. The permits were officially out of sight, out of mind for Justin and Miranda, and they methodically moved forward to the next item that needed their attention; a six-month food supply. As previously mentioned in the "Pacific Crest Trail" section in Chapter 1 of *The 2650 Mile Aisle*, all the food would not be carried with them at once. Instead, the food would be strategically rationed in boxes to send via mail to specific checkpoints of towns they planned to be in at certain times. First of all, Justin and Miranda determined how much food they wanted to carry at once. Obviously, the more food carried, the less shipments they would need to get sent, but that would require a heavier load in their upwards of twenty miles marched on some days. On the other hand, the lighter their food load, the more shipments they would need sent—which isn't always promising as the small towns and outposts are few and far between in the desert, for example. After an objective approach by both of them, Justin and Miranda figured out the perfect balance of the amount of food that needed to be sent periodically, and evidently the amount carried on their backs too. Justin and Miranda precisely calculated the number of calories they would require per day and week, and so on and so forth. In this computation, they also took into consideration the tally of calories they would burn each day and week as well (and I think even minute). Evaluating the proper food supply needed was no easy task—but as always, Justin and Miranda overcame this challenge—as there wasn't any room for error whatsoever. In their quantum-like equation, Justin and Miranda astutely recognized that denser nutrient foods would be more appropriate and most logical for their endeavors. Denser and higher calorie foods would mean two things: less shipments sent, and more space in their backpacks for other supplies and equipment.

To throw another monkey wrench into the equation, Justin's insulin was necessary to account for in the shipments. Bluntly stated, if a diabetic doesn't receive the correct amount of insulin that his/her body needs to function, he/she can lose a limb, go blind, or die. Another twist is that it is vital for insulin to be refrigerated until it's opened for use. The thinking caps were fully utilized as Justin and Miranda reckoned a way around this obstacle, and they discovered a way to keep the insulin cool with mini ice packs. Furthermore, Justin realized through trial-and-error of sorts in Miranda and his previous thru-hikes that the less food he ate and more he exercised—the less insulin his body required to remain at desirable blood glucose levels. He approached this conclusion very cautiously but still used it to his benefit when preparing for the hike. On top of that, can you name a better person for a diabetic to hike with for nearly six months than Miranda? I mean, c'mon, she is a nutritional dietitian. Justin was categorically in the best of hands heading into the trailhead; like it was meant to be.

    Justin and Miranda proceeded extremely systematically as they continued crossing off items of their Pacific Crest Trail preparation checklist. Although receiving the trail permits and assembling an adequate food supply plan was imperative, determining the proper equipment was just as critical to them. Yes, it is true that equipment may seem less important than food or even being allowed on the trail, but Justin and Miranda sustained their 'only as strong as the weakest link' outlook. They viewed every part of the preparation of the Pacific Crest Trail just as important as the hiking of the Pacific Crest Trail itself—always perceiving the parts and whole as one in the same. The contrary to this perspective can be described as a beautiful, aesthetically pleasing Ferrari that has rusted wheels that are rotting away. It doesn't matter how gorgeous the leather on the interior is; or the glistening of the cherry-red exterior in the sunlight; or the souped-up engine under its hood that there are only five of ever made—if the wheels fall off the car a half a mile down the road. In so many words, every part of something is just as important as every other part, and evidently the whole object or thing in general. In Justin and Miranda's case, every single aspect relating to the Pacific Crest Trail was just as pertinent as every other aspect, and ultimately the journey in its entirety. Because of this attitude, their planning of equipment needed for the adventure was meticulously calculated. Whether it was determining the number of hiking shoes they would wear throughout; or finding the lightest possible tents that didn't sacrifice quality or its intended purpose; or considering the various clothing and supplies necessary in the wide range of climates they would face—it was all analyzed and computed accordingly in an exact fashion.

Perfection is practically impossible to maintain, but that didn't deter Justin and Miranda from striving for it. When considering the unpredictability factor of anything in life—but especially the 2650 miles of the Pacific Crest Trail— it is unfeasible to prepare and account ahead of time for all the infinite number of possibilities. Most often in such unforeseeable cases, thinking on the toes with a definitive and confident reaction is the best solution to the incalculable. But with that being said—due to accuracy in thought and precision in action—Justin and Miranda were perfect in the things they could control when planning for the PCT.

The Final Chat

Around the new year, Justin and Miranda visited Pittsburgh one last time before heading to the Pacific Crest trailhead three months afterwards. Our family played our usual board games, hooted and hollered with laughter over nothing in particular, cooked delicious meals, and carried on thought-provoking conversations. It was excellent as always to spend time with them going into the new year. Everything felt normal until the day Justin and Miranda departed back to Michigan, where they would both put in their two-week notices in the coming months. It started to settle in that it would be the last time I would see them until their wedding celebration in October, assuming they returned to Colorado from the Pacific Crest Trail safe and sound. It was an exciting time for them; but unambiguously the unknown was lurking onward, as it always is. As my family and I helped haul their suitcases to the car, we said our usual so-longs. There was an extra sense of compassion in the hugs that were exchanged—due to the unknown—because this time it was magnified more than ever before. Although it wasn't brought to anybody's attention, both our eyes and theirs were glassed over as a powerful smile was bravely glued to all our faces. A few minutes passed as we conversed some more. My last words to Justin and Miranda were, "You guys ready for the hike?" Justin responded very frankly with a confident, fun-loving smirk on his face, "We're ready for an adventure." They hopped in their vehicle and we waved to them as they peeked into the rear-view mirror. After that, we watched them travel forward to the road ahead.

A couple of months later, it was the end of February and Justin and Miranda were departing in under a week for the most southwestern part of the United States to begin the first steps of their grand journey. My phone rang and it was my brother. We chatted for a few minutes about the typical day-to-day stuff; "What are you up to?" "How's the weather up there?" We penetrated the surface soon after into more meaningful subjects as it would be the last time we would speak for a while. I could feel the enthusiasm through the phone as his energy entered my ear and traveled all the way down my body—through my veins and ribcage—to the soles of my feet and out my toes. I wasn't sure if he was about to go to an amusement park or begin a 2650-mile quest.

As we continued our heart-to-heart, I felt it was an appropriate time to reciprocate a dose of inspiration his way for good measure to keep in Miranda and his back pocket for the next six months. For the first time, I mentioned that the bracelet gifted from Miranda in California continued to be around my wrist and explained the reason it was still there. He appreciated the expression of gratitude but soon tactically deflected it as his humility usually leads him to do regarding any form of praise.

Our conversation glided along as I provoked him to further touch on the origin of how the idea of hiking the Pacific Crest Trail arose. He mentioned how Miranda initially surfaced the radical potentiality. Justin said to me, "We love the wilderness and are satisfied with where we are at in life, yet Miranda and I haven't been exceedingly delighted in our current situation as of late. This is something that really electrified us. After calculating everything involved with hiking the trail—such as knowing it's the only time to do so since we are still young, the financial aspect of continuing payments on student loans, insurance, food, etc. adding up; as well as the legitimacy of moving to Colorado afterwards—we made our definitive decision and didn't look back since." He went on to say, "A traditional lifestyle doesn't excite me."

I inquired about how his boss took the news of him leaving the company out of the blue, as my brother was slated to replace the senior engineer retiring at the end of the year. He explained how his boss wished it wasn't the case, but he granted Justin the best of luck in Miranda and his future endeavors. His former boss also affirmatively stated that Justin always had a place at the company if he ever returned to Michigan. I asked Justin what his co-workers and friends thought of the unconventional trek. He noted that he refrained from telling people about it unless they directly inquired. Although when the topic did surface, he said that others were usually rather bewildered as to why. Justin's keeping of Miranda and his hike to himself came to no surprise to me, but it spoke volumes hearing this because it confirmed the fact that Justin and Miranda were embarking on the 2650-mile journey for nobody else but themselves.

In our final chat, Justin was genuinely curious how I was doing, as if I was the one with the extensive adventure ahead; although every single adventure both big and small were viewed with the same grandeur in his eyes. Eventually, the discussion shifted back onto his side of the court when I asked him, in so many words, the very general question, "How do you do it?" I remember Justin responded very succinctly and thoughtfully by saying, "Figure out what you really want and then get it." He rephrased that same point by stating, "Set a goal and then achieve it." The conciseness and potency of his words resonated with me. Regarding the lifestyle that Miranda and he live, Justin remarked, "We could save money all year for a three-week vacation or instead hike freely every weekend and go for a run or be outdoors after work." Their 'work to live; not live to work' philosophy flashed in my mind immediately upon Justin saying that. Also returning to me was the discussion Justin, my dad, and I had the last time he was in Pennsylvania a couple months prior when the age-old question of,

"What would you do if you won the lottery?" was posed. Without hesitation, Justin decided that if he won the lottery (although he never played), he would "Buy a nice cargo van, like one with some comfortable sleeping space, and travel around the United States for a few years in it."

Later on in our final conversation over the phone—in Justin's final reflective and insightful riff before the Pacific Crest Trail—he added, "That nobody should ever feel sorry for themselves and that it can always be worse." Justin continued, "Even if in the worst place in life, the past is set and the only thing that can be controlled are the steps moving forward to get out of the situation." We spoke for a few more minutes and Justin digressed by affirmatively declaring, "Life is a series of actions and reactions. And that the only thing that can be controlled is the reaction."

He and I exchanged our last words of compassion and best wishes—as I'm sure he could hear the smile oozing from my face—and we ended the call. As I sat in silence for a few moments, I couldn't help but illuminate with life from Justin and my final chat.

The adventurers at heart were now prepared for the adventure of a lifetime. Throughout Justin and Miranda's stimulating experiences—from Europe to the Grand Canyon, and running half-marathons to the trip out west, among many other occurrences—each of their senses of self were realized and refined in each conscious adventure. From the grandest of events to the most trivial of day-to-day activities, a truth persists with Justin and Miranda: Full attention is granted to the task at hand and they become one with it.

In their eyes, the trip to Europe was the best adventure they ever had. In their eyes, the Detroit/Windsor Half-Marathon was the best adventure they ever had. In their eyes, the trip to the Grand Canyon was the best adventure they ever had. In their eyes, driving to the grocery store was the best adventure they ever had. In their eyes, making freshly ground French Press coffee in Michigan when the sun was just rising was the best adventure they ever had. In their eyes, sitting still with all the wildlife on their back porch in Michigan—drinking that same cup of French Press coffee—was the best adventure they ever had. And in their eyes, I'm sure the Pacific Crest Trail will be the best adventure they ever had too. The Grand Canyon, in addition to prompting enhanced self-realization for Justin and Miranda, also opened their eyes to the perpetual realization of the grander scheme of life. Justin captured this paradoxical, rather indescribable meaning when he said this on a different social media post following Miranda and his engagement: "The feeling of standing there in a land of nothing next to my everything is a moment tough to describe yet impossible to forget. The energy amidst stillness, the world going on up there while we were in

THE 2650 MILE AISLE

complete solitude down here." And as if they weren't aware of it before each one of their adventures that was more challenging than the preceding one, Justin and Miranda are now more certain than ever that Mother Nature always welcomes them to her home—which is also their home. They view every day as an adventure through nature, whether it's at the office or in the mountains. As Justin and Miranda have leveled up and continue to progress and up the ante with every single one of their adventures, the most towering hike to date stares them in the face—the Pacific Crest Trail.

    A couple of weeks before Justin and Miranda left for their excursion, something magnificent occurred. Due to complications with iCloud sharing on Justin and my phones, our apps and notes link from time to time. As I tapped the notepad application in my phone to jot down some thoughts, I was inadvertently defaulted into Justin's note which had just been written. It was the day before Miranda and he departed on their journey. Before I realized what was before my eyes, I was already engulfed in one of the most moving passages have ever read. I put two and two together that Justin was the individual responsible for such powerful words. The dialogue that was in Justin's notes was eventually attached to his social media post the next day (the starting day of the quest), so I am more comfortable sharing it since it was not meant to be a private account. The brilliant and expressive message in Justin's virtual notebook and social media caption—as Miranda and he embraced in the photo—in its entirety was:

Standing at the Southern Terminus of the Pacific Crest Trail letting the immensity of the 2650-mile adventure that lies ahead of us sink in, I also reflect on the journey that got us here. Many sacrifices were made to bring this crazy dream of ours to fruition. We've left our jobs and friends in Michigan, will miss out on graduations, weddings, and be away from our families and cat for months not knowing what the next day holds. While all of that excites primal emotions of fear and anxiety, we are comforted by the love and support of our family/friends, our health, and most importantly each other. So in a way, I feel accomplished before we even take our first step on the trail. Making it to Canada is a goal, but it is certainly not the destination.

There is no telling what these next few months will bring, and that is fine by me. We will persevere not by living in the past or the future, only grounded in the present moment.

Happy Trails

CHAPTER 8: CONCLUSION

The Uncontrollable Virus

This specific portion of Walt Whitman's brilliant poem, *Leaves of Grass*, reminds me of Justin and Miranda and is a perfect way to begin the "Conclusion" of *The 2650 Mile Aisle*:

>Long enough have you dreamed contemptible dreams,
>Now I wash the gum from your eyes,
>You must habit yourself to the dazzle of the light and of every
>moment of our life.

>Long have you timidly waited, holding a plank by the shore,
>Now I will you to be a bold swimmer,
>To jump off in the midst of the sea, and rise again and nod to me and
>shout, and laughingly dash with your hair.[1]

Indeed, Justin and Miranda habit themselves to every moment of their lives. And as bold swimmers (hikers), they are embarking on the 2650-mile traverse of the Pacific Crest Trail—jumping off in the midst of the sea—sure to rise again. The decision to quit their jobs to bravely dive head first into the unknown sea that is the Pacific Crest Trail is simply another realization of their courage and willingness to push the limits of life. Around a week into March, Justin and Miranda took the leap of faith, commencing the hike at the Southern Terminus trailhead and didn't even think about looking back.

Life is uncertain; there is no question about it. It is forever flowing onward, and no one truly knows what's around the next bend. There are endless surprises big and small in our everyday lives that are unimaginable. But as Justin elegantly said in our final chat before Miranda and he started their newest adventure, "Life is a series of actions and reactions. And that the only thing that can be controlled is the reaction."

Now, due to perhaps the granddaddy surprise of them all, Justin and Miranda were required to put their reactionary mindsets into practice. A couple of weeks into their hiking of the Pacific Crest Trail, an extremely contagious and deadly virus was spreading not only around the United States—but the entire world. COVID-19, or coronavirus, can cause severe respiratory complications. It affects the nose, sinuses, throat,

THE 2650 MILE AISLE

and especially the lungs. COVID-19 can be deadly for anybody, but even more so for individuals with pre-existing conditions, such as asthma, heart disease—diabetes—and much more.[2] The disease was spreading across the United States and world at an alarming rate, so nearly every state in the United States issued a state of emergency announcement as well as a stay-at-home order for all its citizens to quarantine. This meant that nobody could leave their house unless it was for essential items, such as groceries or to pick up a prescription from the pharmacy. Due to the pandemic, the Pacific Crest Trail Association (PCTA) recommended that all hikers leave the trail immediately. There were no ands, ifs, or buts about it as no one was advised to be on the trail until further notice—as Justin and Miranda were just short of the 200-mile marker at that point.

When we heard the unfortunate news from Justin and Miranda, obviously they weren't jumping for joy—but they also weren't as torn as we originally expected—as it was apparent that they accepted the situation for what it was. They refused to look backwards at something that couldn't be changed to sulk, pout, or complain. Instead, they looked forward as to how to make the best out of the situation at hand, and the adversity they were facing that was putting a halt to something that they dedicated themselves to and planned for tirelessly. Justin and Miranda decided they would play it by ear and head back to

Miranda's mom's place in Arizona until they received the okay from the trail association to return to the PCT—which was not guaranteed, as the virus and its spread was in control at that point. When planning to hike 2650 miles into the wilderness—water, food, dangerous animals, hypothermia, proper equipment, drowning, trees falling, among many other risks and obstacles were considered and accounted for—but certainly not a global pandemic viciously thrusting itself in the way.

Whatever one may call the circumstances that stared Justin and Miranda in the face, they were what they were. The only possible thing Justin and Miranda were able to do was respond to the situation at hand, and they did so with clear eyes and full hearts. Their intended adventure and the way they accepted the uncertain impediment also reminds me of lines from the same *Leaves of Grass* poem from the onset of this chapter:

> *This is the thrill of a thousand clear cornets and scream of the octave*
> *flute and strike of triangles.*

> *I play not a march or victors only . . . I play great marches for con-*
> *quered and slain persons.*

> *Have you heard that it was good to gain the day?*

THE 2650 MILE AISLE

> *I also say it is good to fall . . . battles are lost in the same spirit in which*
> > *they are won.*
>
> *I sound triumphal drums for the dead . . . I fling through my*
> > *embouchures the loudest and gayest music to them,*
> > *Vivas to those who have failed, and to those whose war-vessels sank*
> > > *in the sea, and those themselves who sank in the sea,*
> > *And to all generals that lost engagements, and all overcome heroes,*
> > > *and the numberless unknown heroes equal to the greatest heroes*
> > > > *known"*[3]

Undoubtedly, this battle of Justin and Miranda was lost in the same spirit it would be won. Although the battle may be surrendered, I am certain they will win the war. This massive setback—although appearing not as grand in Justin and Miranda's eyes—will prove to be only a pebble in the way of their immense trail of life. Throughout this seemingly detrimental happening of the global pandemic, they continued to remain unflappable. For the time being, they will sojourn in Arizona patiently—awaiting a promising message from the PCTA—but in the meantime, living life and staying active, as we will see in the next section. The "thrill of a thousand clear cornets and scream of the octave flute and strike of triangles" will keep sounding for Justin and Miranda as they will bend yet never break, always satisfied in their grander journey. Justin precisely pointed toward this fact in the note he jotted prior to the trail when he said, "So in a way I feel accomplished before we even take our first step on the trail. Making it to Canada is a goal, but it is certainly not the destination."

Justin and Miranda's potent spirit of life inside of their bodies leads them to an arrival at their destination in every step—in the present moment. The "triumphal drums" will continue to blare as Justin and Miranda continue their march onwards. When regarding the uncontrollable virus causing their removal from the Pacific Crest Trail—or any manifestation of adversity in their lives—they are unerringly aware of the one thing they can control; their reaction.

But They Can't Be Taken Away from Adventure

Justin and Miranda's reaction to the virus was one filled to the brim with life, as they certainly weren't going to stop living it. They were conscious that it was going to progress forward no matter what they did, so it was wise to merge with the procession. In that way, they would advance themselves as life was also advancing. Justin and Miranda's stream ahead could have whirled them two ways: positively or negatively. They chose to actively float in the former of these options.

Although restrained from the Pacific Crest Trail, their positive response kept them hiking along. In quarantine, instead of spending their precious time staring at the wall, unproductive, and bored; Justin and Miranda wrung the most life out of their PCT lapse by hiking portions of the Arizona Trail. With all the supplies, equipment, and trail necessities at their disposal, they have been hiking roughly 80 miles per week of the Arizona Trail, returning to Miranda's mom's place for the weekend—only to trek another leg the following Monday through Friday. On the weekends, Justin and Miranda are spending their time doing yoga on the rooftop or cooking their debut recipe of homemade pasta—as they were always ready to ignite the ember inside of them.

When I spoke to Justin and Miranda over the phone, they were hopeful to return to the Pacific Crest Trail if permitted but were prepared if that didn't come to fruition. They were equally satisfied marching along the Arizona Trail as they would have been reinstating themselves on the Pacific Crest Trail; or making homemade pasta; or creating a make-shift yoga class; or watching a movie; or going for a run; or simply vibrantly doing nothing. They knew life was ceaselessly flowing, and they weren't going to stand in its way. Justin and Miranda let its gust carry their sails to where they needed to be.

The glorious balance between stillness and progression; they were impartially satisfied with both. Everything in Justin and Miranda's perspective was viewed as delightful and beautiful and graceful—or else none of it would be. No, leaving the Pacific Crest Trail was not in Justin and Miranda's inital itinerary, but it wasn't going to stop them from embracing, surfing, and caressing the endless wave of unknowns ahead in the ocean of life. Yes, adventure can be taken away from Justin and Miranda. But no, they can't be taken away from adventure.

The Best Man

The best man, on the surface, is a brother or close friend to somebody who is getting married. But in reality—beyond its particular form—the best man's essence and power is much deeper, grander, and magnificent than at first it may seem. It is the shining light of truth that is within everyone. Being the best man is something that is in reach evidently to Justin and Miranda, and you, and me, and to all—regardless of a wedding celebration or not. We are all capable of being dubbed the best man.

Being the best man to you surely means something slightly different than it means to me in a certain situation—and Justin and Miranda as well. Being the best man means being a better man or woman today, right now—than you were yesterday—or even moments ago. It is the perpetual honorable and graceful battle, one that has been here since time immemorial. Being the best man is a conscious choice. It is imperative one is being the best man rather than becoming the best man—a mere illusion—a distant day that may not ever manifest in reality. Being the best man is not a means to an end but an end in itself. Being the best man is timeless, formless, and attainable. Using the power within, we have the spirit and grace to be the best man right now. Whether it be seemingly the most trivial of conversations or matters of the grandest action—they are equally worthy—and I challenge you, the reader, to be the best man therein always. Being the best man is the essence of life, something that will certainly not die. But remember being the best man is enough—it is complete in itself—just as the act of hiking the Pacific Crest Trail is satisfactory on its own. The trail was never a means to an end either. The journey, adventure, experience, and wisdom gained throughout by Justin and Miranda—or you and me on another symbolic trail—is sufficient on its own. Being the best man is noble in itself. Each of us all, no matter how we arrive here, need not to look anywhere but within ourselves—to truly be the best man.

When entrenched in a rut of my lower energy state and boyish mind and spirit, I often remind myself of Justin and Miranda. That spark of light encourages me to look inward at the undivided married self, and find the best man waiting there for me. The best man is then again united as one, forever patient of your and my arrival. Justin and Miranda's character and relationship absolutely inspired this book, encouraging me to delve deeper into what makes them who they are—and why they do what they do. But true inspiration isn't emulating or idolizing anyone or anything. True inspiration allows one to look inward and see the power that's been latent all along, thus activating it to its full potential. Inspiration is enough in itself; it is an end of the old and a beginning of the new. Inspiration is inside all of us ready to give and receive freely—but we just

THE 2650 MILE AISLE

need to be prompted sometimes; or change our views to a different angle; or elevate and enhance our perspectives. The best man in Justin and Miranda undoubtedly inspires the best man in myself.

As Justin and Miranda have shown how to be the best man and woman, be the best man in your own life; not compared to other people but the best version of yourself. That is the meaning of the best man in its purest form. For Justin and Miranda, the hike on the Pacific Crest Trail is just one step and realization of this grander journey. I urge you to find your own Pacific Crest Trail. It is one thing to think how to be the best man—it is another to be the best man. With all of this being said, no matter where life takes you in your own journey—or you take it—be your own best man.

CAMERON JAMES WILLIAMS

You May Now Kiss the Bride

But I plead you not to take these words or any words to heart without finding the meaning out for yourself. The Bible, Quran, Buddhist teachings, any religious text, poetry, science, art—and *The 2650 Mile Aisle*—all point to this indescribable thing. Except, simply, that's all they do. This thing has no name and can only be felt—as if there is any such word that can embody its fullness—since it is in everything in life forever. This thing progresses forward each day for all the days—or else the working man wouldn't be able to feel ill and call in sick, or show up for his duty when he is healthy again; or the family wouldn't be able to take the vacation to the beach; or the scientist wouldn't be able to develop her theory; or the baby wouldn't be able to cry interminably in her carriage; or Justin and Miranda, or you and me, wouldn't be—if not the case, then none of it would be. It is the nameless thing that doesn't come and go. Living how Justin and Miranda live is an endless and constant practice; one that was always here, is here now, and will continue to be here. The closing lines of *Horatius at the Bridge* are:

> *With weeping and with laughter*
> *Still is the story told,*
> *How well Horatius kept the bridge*
> *In the brave days of the old.*[1]

THE 2650 MILE AISLE

For Horatius, and Justin, and Miranda, their chronicles may come to a closure here—but what's inside of them doesn't end—as the story continues onward. Fortunately, due to the removal of certain quarantine regulations, Justin and Miranda have returned to the Pacific Crest Trail. But whether or not they finish the hike before the wedding celebration in October is of minor importance here. Yes, this is the end of *Horatius of the Bridge* and *The 2650 Mile Aisle*, but it is only the beginning of something new, of further metaphoric bridges to *keep* and hikes to embark on.

All of these words written are merely a symbol of the meaning and feeling encompassed within them. Justin and Miranda are also symbols of sorts—being emphasized to instill the utmost meaning—while every single one of their exploits remaining true. The feelings I felt from the experiences depicted that were then translated and encapsulated into written form, and favorably the feelings of you, the reader, is akin to the feelings of hearing birds chirp on a sunny Sunday morning; or standing outside at night in complete stillness, delightfully gazing up at the moon, stars, and infinite Universe without a single thought on the mind; or watching a child innocently smile carefree while licking ice cream off of a cone without a worry in the world; or the mother experiencing that same child miraculously born from the depths of nothing.

Repetitive points from different angles have been made around the theme but it is imperative to make the supreme essence clear. Some call it being aligned with God; others Allah; others Krishna; others Life; others the Universe; others the Soul; others Being; others Presence; others Love; others Truth; others Consciousness; or perhaps some don't call it anything at all. Regardless, it is inexpressible, intangible, and manifests itself into infinite forms here right now endlessly. Whatever the case, all streams end up at the ocean—as there are countless ways to draw the radius of a circle.

And as these sixty thousand plus words are written, there is still more to say describing Justin and Miranda's character and what makes them live life. Likely, this is because what is inside of them—and you and me—is indescribable and no amount of words are sufficient. These symbols of words, and examples, and stories only point towards the direction of this nameless source. They can be used to show the way but that is only the half. The steps need to continue to be taken by Justin, and Miranda, and you, and me, and any being of life—as every trail is different but all of them lead to the same arrival. This portal of life is for all from the East to the West; young to the old; poor to the rich; and ill to the healthy. As we've seen, Justin and Miranda are well aware of this truth, manifesting it with courage; with confidence; with grace living satisfied in the present moment; with willingness to push the limits of life while progressing forward;

with strength to face the unknown head-on; with honor to conquer adversity; and with beauty in togetherness, not only with each other but also within themselves.

Now, Justin—without further ado—you may now kiss the bride.

CAMERON JAMES WILLIAMS

REFERENCES

CHAPTER 1: INTRODUCTION
Justin and Miranda at the Bridge
1. Babington, *Horatius at the Bridge,* 1904, Lines 1-17, 65-81, 130-157, 213-240, 249-252, 586-589, https://www.bartleby.com/360/7/158.html.

2. Emerson, *Self-Reliance,* 1841, Paragraph 14, https://literarydevices.net/to-be-great-is-to-be-misunderstood/.

The Announcement
1. Teamsoul, "I Am Fearless Soul", Fearless Soul, June 22, 2016, https://iamfearlesssoul.com/if-you-change-the-way-you-look-at-things-the-things-you-look-at-change/.

The Pacific Crest Trail
1. Cruz Bay Publishing, "Backpacker", https://www.backpacker.com/trips/long-trails/pacific-crest-trail.

2,3,5. "Pacific Crest Trail Association", Pacific Crest Trail Association, https://www.pcta.org/discover-the-trail/.

4. Bland, "Smithsonian Mag", *Smithsonian Magazine*, April 8, 2013, https://www.smithsonianmag.com/travel/going-the-distance-on-the-pacific-crest-trail-17459480/.

6,7. Mac, "Halfway Anywhere", Halfway Anywhere, https://www.halfwayanywhere.com/trails/pacific-crest-trail/17-things-scarier-than-bears-on-the-pacific-crest-trail/.

8. Poehler, "USA Today Nation", *USA Today*, published October 19, 2019; updated October 20, 2019, https://www.usatoday.com/story/news/nation/2019/10/19/pacific-crest-trail-hiker-found-after-getting-lost-oregon-snowstorm/4042122002/.

9. Jostad, "Crabtree Meadows", High Sierra Hikers, http://www.highsierrahikers.org/ranger_reports/1999CrabtreeJostad.pdf.

10. Stickney, "NBC San Diego", *NBC San Diego*, July 28, 2014, https://www.nbcsandiego.com/news/local/death-of-teenager-along-pacific-crest-trail-ruled-an-accident/1994660/.

11. Cowan, "The San Diego Union-Tribune North County", *San Diego Union-Tribune*, August 5, 2017, https://www.sandiegouniontribune.com/communities/north-county/sd-no-cowan-column-0805-story.html.

12. Strayed, *Wild: A Journey from Lost to Found*, January 1, 2013, https://www.amazon.com/Wild-Journey-Found-CHERYL-STRAYED/dp/0857897756.

/////"PART 1: PRE-MIRANDA"/////
Where It All Started
1. Schembechler, "AZ Quotes", AZ Quotes, https://www.azquotes.com/quote/754065.

CHAPTER 2: RESPECT IS EARNED; NOT GIVEN
The Williams Name
1. Kuran, *Private Truths, Public Lies*, September 30, 1997, https://www.hup.harvard.edu/catalog.php?isbn=9780674707580.

2. Sinha, "Search Quotes", Search Quotes, https://www.searchquotes.com/quotation/One_who_is_transparent_in_words_%26_action%2C_commands_confidence_%26_respect._He_takes_decision_with_stre/736928/.

CHAPTER 3: A MAN AS A BOY
Introductory Words
1. Proctor, "Good Reads", Good Reads, https://www.goodreads.com/quotes/4472945-the-only-limits-in-our-life-are-those-we-impose.

Pushing the Limits of Intellect
1. Einstein, "Good Reads", Good Reads, https://www.goodreads.com/quotes/19421-if-you-can-t-explain-it-to-a-six-year-old.

2. Ritchie, "Quote Investigator", Quote Investigator, https://quoteinvestigator.com/2015/08/28/fish/.

3. Socrates quoted, in *Apology* by Plato, dialogue set in 399 BCE, https://www.shmoop.com/quotes/i-only-know-that-i-know-nothing.html.

CHAPTER 4: THE ONLY WAY IS THROUGH
Introductory Words
1. Royal Air Force, 1912, https://enacademic.com/dic.nsf/enwiki/2053250.

2. American Heritage Dictionary, s.v. "Newton's third law", https://www.ahdictionary.com/word/search.html?q=Newton%27s+third+law.

3. Hill, edited and annotated by Lechter, *Outwitting the Devil: The Secret to Freedom and Success,* Inside Cover, September 18, 2012.

4. Hill, edited and annotated by Lechter, *Outwitting the Devil: The Secret to Freedom and Success,* Back of Book Synopsis, September 18, 2012.

The Blemish Never Seen
1. Tzu, "Good Reads", Good Reads, https://www.goodreads.com/quotes/193920-because-one-believes-in-oneself-one-doesn-t-try-to-convince.

2. Lincoln, "Address to gathering of entrepreneurs and farmers in Wisconsin", 1859, https://leadershipwatch-aadboot.com/2019/09/21/this-too-shall-pass-said-lincoln-and-what-it-means-for-leadership-today/.

Concluding Remarks
1. Hill, Lechter, Reid, *Three Feet From Gold: Turn Your Obstacles into Opportunities!,* January 1, 2019, https://www.selfhelpdaily.com/napoleon-hills-three-feet-from-gold/.

2. Michelangelo, "Brainy Quote", Brainy Quote, https://www.brainyquote.com/quotes/michelangelo_183563.

3. Van Gogh, "Brainy Quote", Brainy Quote, https://www.brainyquote.com/quotes/vincent_van_gogh_384252.

CHAPTER 5: NEW BEGINNINGS
Introductory Words
1. Twain, "Twain Quotes", Twain Quotes, http://www.twainquotes.com/Discovery.html.

Fall Seven Times, Stand Up Eight
1. Proverbs 24:16 (King James Version) https://www.quotescosmos.com/bible/bible-quotes/Fall-seven-times-stand-up-eight-Proverbs-24-16.html.

////Part 2: POST-MIRANDA////
Introductory Words
1. Lexico Powered by Oxford, s.v. "marriage", https://www.lexico.com/en/definition/marriage.

2. "Blog", Mckinley Irvin, October 30, 2012; updated 2018, https://www.mckinleyirvin.com/family-law-blog/2012/october/32-shocking-divorce-statistics/.

3,4,5.6,7. Hill, *Think and Grow Rich*, 1937, Pages 249-53.

CHAPTER 6: A MATCH MADE IN (WHATEVER YOUR BELIEF SYSTEM)

Welcome to the Party, Miranda
1. Ali, "Brainy Quote", Brainy Quote, https://www.brainyquote.com/quotes/muhammad_ali_125243.

2. Ali, "Good Reads", Good Reads, https://www.goodreads.com/quotes/121392-he-who-is-not-courageous-enough-to-take-risks-will.

Winter Break: Plus One Edition
1. Aristotle, "Journalism at Bucks", Bucks, http://faculty.bucks.edu/rogerst/jour275morals.htm.

Miranda Meet Justin; Justin Meet Miranda
1. Tolle, *A New Earth: Awakening to Your Life's Purpose*, January 30, 2008, Pages 265-266.

Acquired Taste
1. Einstein, "Good Reads", Good Reads, https://www.goodreads.com/quotes/19421-if-you-can-t-explain-it-to-a-six-year-old.

2. "Techopedia", Techopedia, February 5, 2019, https://www.techopedia.com/definition/20262/keep-it-simple-stupid-principle-kiss-principle.

3. Whitehouse, "Sci-Tech", *BBC News*, November 15, 2000, http://news.bbc.co.uk/2/hi/science/nature/1024779.stm.

Concluding Remarks
1. Lexico Powered by Oxford, s.v. "togetherness", https://www.lexico.com/en/definition/togetherness.

2. "Walt Whitman", Poetry Foundation, https://www.poetryfoundation.org/poets/walt-whitman.

3. Whitman, *Leaves of Grass*, 1855, Page 108.

CHAPTER 7: ADVENTURERS AT HEART
Introductory Words
1. Van Vynckt, "Livestrong", Livestrong, https://www.livestrong.com/article/435265-why-do-you-need-to-drink-a-lot-of-water-at-a-high-altitude/.

2. Thoreau, *Walden Pond*, 1854, Page 92.

3. Tolkien, *The Fellowship of the Ring*, 1954, Page 182.

Broadening Their Horizons
1. Directed by Gus Van Sant, Written by Matt Damon and Ben Affleck, Robin Williams and Matt

Damon in scene, *Good Will Hunting,* (Park Bench Scene), 1997.

Run, Justin (Forrest), Run
1. Directed by Robert Zemeckis, Quote by Tom Hanks, *Forrest Gump,* 1994, https://www.quotes.net/mquote/33529.

No Plan B
1. "El Capitan", Alex Honnold, http://www.alexhonnold.com/.

2. Fimrite, "Nation and World", *The Seattle Times,* June 10, 2018, updated June 11, 2018, https://www.seattletimes.com/nation-world/witness-describes-death-plunge-of-two-yosemite-climbers/.

The Bracelet
1. Luke 10:25-37 (New International Version), *The Parable of the Good Samaritan.*

CHAPTER 8: CONCLUSION
The Uncontrollable Virus
1. Whitman, *Leaves of Grass,* 1855, Page 64.

2. Gillespie, "Health", Health, March 17, 2020, https://www.health.com/condition/infectious-diseases/coronavirus/coronavirus-preexisting-conditions.

3. Whitman, *Leaves of Grass*, 1855, Page 34.

You May Now Kiss the Bride
1. Babington, *Horatius at the Bridge*, 1904, Lines 586-589,
https://www.bartleby.com/360/7/158.html.

ACKNOWLEDGEMENTS

There are too many people to thank and acknowledge as anyone ever in my life has had some sort of positive impact on me, whether directly or indirectly. These acknowledgements will attempt to stick to those who have directly guided, influenced, or have helped me transcend my own portal in life.

First and foremost, I want to thank my family. I have the best family I could possibly imagine. With love and support, we are all each other's best friends. Thank you for respecting my space when drafting the manuscript of *The 2650 Mile* Aisle. Thank you, Mom and Dad for raising Justin, Alexa, Abbey, and I to be able to stand on our own two feet and think for ourselves at all times.

Mom, I appreciate your hard work and perseverance through life; you are a sweet soul. You have always been an integral part of my life and nothing has changed to this day.

Dad, I love talking with you about absolutely anything. I can't even begin to express the gratitude I have for the positive impact you have made and continue to make on my life. I appreciate your hard work and perseverance in life as well your ability to be satisfied with the little things in life; you have shown me how to enjoy life and all its beauty. I truly couldn't ask for better parents to welcome me to life.

Justin, I'm going to keep these words short and sweet as this whole book was about you. But, "Thanks for being a true braj, braj."

Alexa, as my older sister you have also inspired me to live life to its fullest sense. Your determination and fun-loving nature are some of the things I appreciate about you. You fearlessly walk in and out of the hospital each day to help people. That is commendable as it gets. Abbey couldn't ask for a better sister.

Abbey, while we're here, thank you for being the best little sister a brother could have. Our bond is second to none. One day you may be there to make me laugh, while the next day you may be an open ear willing to listen or give advice. (remember, we're a package deal) Keep shining your bright light onto this world. You are a beautiful soul.

And Jake, you're the sweetest beagle on the block (and maybe the loudest). No matter how much you stepped on the laptop when I was trying to work—your cuteness, innocence, and playfulness will always make it impossible to not stop what I'm doing to love and pet you.

Words don't begin to serve justice on how wonderful and appreciative I am of my family. Thank you all for everything. Love yinz!

To the Huiting family, thank you for being yourselves. I am forever appreciative of the outstanding Huiting family hospitality when my family and I visited Colorado.

Miranda, I will also keep this portion short and sweet as well since you and Justin were the focal points of *The 2650 Mile* Aisle. Thank you being yourself and thinking for yourself. I'm glad to be able to call you my sister-in-law.

I am eager to give a huge thank you to the editor of this piece of writing, Caryn Pine. You helped turn the initial manuscript of *The 2650 Mile Aisle* into the final product, which is something I will always be grateful for. Thank you for your undying support and encouragement as well your phenomenal skillset to refine the manuscript into its best possible form. *The 2650 Mile Aisle* would not have happened without you. There aren't enough words to show my appreciation for you.

My friend, William L. Douglas, also known as Guardian of the 'Horn Undershelf, and also known

CAMERON JAMES WILLIAMS

as Bill, thank you for introducing me to the profoundly splendid poem, *Horatius at the Bridge*. I also can't forget to mention your political, financial, or philosophical quotes which always brightened my day.

And my appreciation also goes to Robert, an author I met at the mall. He and I then went onto converse for over two hours, all while never speaking before that point. Thank you, Robert for inadvertently helping to water the seed of the spirit of writing inside of me. Although a seemingly trivial conversation, *The 2650 Mile Aisle* would have never formulated if it wasn't for you.

Also, I place Mathematician and Economist, Eric Weinstein in an extremely high regard. He, and more precisely his intellectual and thought-provoking podcast "The Portal", have had a deep, positive influence on my entire life and effectually *The 2650 Mile Aisle*.

And once again, thank you Justin and Miranda simply for being yourselves. Keep on living, keep on pushing forward, and keep on being delighted in the present moment.

And last, but certainly not least, my purest of love and gratitude remain with the Universe, the Creator. You have always guided this mind, body, and spirit and continue to guide them exactly to the places necessary for the soul in this body to grow. Even when I doubt, you continue to lead me back on track. Your endless abundance of love, light, and life remain forever in this present being. Thank you for this gift of guidance in all of life's journey and certainly the direction rendered during the journey of writing The 2650 Mile Aisle.

www.ingramcontent.com/pod-product-compliance
Lightning Source LLC
Chambersburg PA
CBHW070528090426
42735CB00013B/2897